A Variorum Edition

of

Elizabeth Barrett Browning's

Sonnets from the Portuguese

A Variorum Edition

of

Elizabeth Barrett Browning's

Sonnets from the Portuguese

by

Miroslava Wein Dow

The Whitston Publishing Company
Troy, New York
1980

PR
4189
A1
1980b

Copyright 1980
Miroslava Wein Dow

ISBN 0-87875-179-3

Printed in the United States of America

For my father, Miroslav Wein

Acknowledgments

Professor William S. Peterson of the University of Maryland pointed out to me the need for a new, complete variorum edition of these poems, and was most generous with his help in seeing me through the task, originally a doctoral dissertation. I am also grateful to Professors Shirley Kenny and Samuel Brown, also of Maryland, for their careful and critical reading of my edition, and for their many helpful suggestions.

I am grateful to Mr. Arthur Houghton, Jr. for his permission to use the Houghton MS, to John Murray, Esq. for permission to use the British Library MS, and to the Trustees of the Pierpont Morgan Library for their permission to use their MS of *Sonnets from the Portuguese.*

I am much obliged to the following publishers for permission to use material from their publications: The Belknap Press of Harvard University Press, Copyright © 1969 by the President and Fellows of Harvard College: for Elvan Kintner's *The Letters of Robert Browning and Elizabeth Barrett Barrett 1845-1846;* John Murray: Thurman L. Hood's *Letters of Robert Browning Collected by Thomas J. Wise;* Harcourt, Brace, Jovanovich: *The Common Reader,* Series Two, by Virginia Woolf; Faber and Faber, Inc.: *Mrs. Browning: A Poet's Work and Its Setting* by Alethea Hayter; Yale University Press: *New Letters of Robert Browning* edited by de Vane and Knickerbocker, and *The Life of Elizabeth Barrett Browning* by Gardner Taplin.

I used photocopies by courtesy of the British Library, the Library of Congress, The Harvard University Library, and Mr. Arthur Houghton, Jr.

Miroslava Dow

CRITICAL INTRODUCTION

Soon after the *Sonnets from the Portuguese* appeared, they were recognized as the personal and particular statement they are. One critic has even complained of feeling like a voyeur in reading them. Fortunately, this degree of decorum is not shared by the thousands of readers who have enjoyed these poems since 1850. While no one now claims the highest honors for the *Sonnets,* almost everyone agrees that there is great beauty and power in them.

Elizabeth Barrett Barrett had served a long apprenticeship before she achieved the consistent excellence of form we recognize in the *Sonnets.* All her life she read and admired Petrarch, Shakespeare, and Wordsworth, and long before she began this sonnet sequence in 1845, she had written sonnets on many subjects. It is the content of the *Sonnets* which marks a radical departure from her previous work. It is the only poetry in which she writes about her own strong and very personal feelings. It is the first of her successful major works, and it is a mature and considerable achievement.

Until she met Robert Browning, E.B.B.'s strongest feelings were religious and familial, although she was an affectionate and loyal friend to those who became her intimates. For the first twenty-six years of her life she led a sheltered country existence, equally repelled by county socializing and by traditional female occupations. During those years she was nourished by her love for her family, particularly her brother Edward, by books, by the countryside, and her friendship with the Greek scholar, Hugh Stuart Boyd. In London, while she read and contributed to the leading reviews, she became increasingly more reclusive as a result of her debilitating illness.

These circumstances—isolation, illness and its attendant addiction to morphine—combined with a strong Nonconformist background and wide reading in the classics as well as in contemporary works, gave her mind a peculiar, sometimes contradictory cast. Virginia Woolf judged her mind as essentially satirical and absorbed by the secular events of her time. It is also evident, however, that E.B.B. was profoundly religious and looked at life with the eyes of one in whom the sharper edges of Nonconformism had been smoothed by a happy life in Catholic Italy. That was to be later; before that time her spiritual orientation sometimes led her into the common pieties and "sentiments" of her time. She was, for example, an ardent admirer of George Sand, whose books she devoured and whom she called "large-brained woman and large-hearted man." While she eagerly read the books she called them "impure" and exhorted Sand to clean them up so that "infants" and "maidens" could touch them with impunity. Many of the early poems abound with saccharine religion and dead lovers. They lack the controlled passion and "truth" of poetry rooted in human experience.

There is the album poetry of sentimental verse; "Rhyme of the Duchess May," "The Romaunt of the Page," "The Lady of the Brown Rosarie" are examples of the genre. There are two rather declamatory religious epics, *The Seraphim* and *A Dream of Exile,* and many other poems on religious subjects. Another large group of poems has religious overtones; religion in these is not always in the matrix of the poetry but is sometimes wheeled on stage at the end. An example of these poems is "A Vision of Poets," in which a young poet is taught that he must share in human suffering in order to be an artist:

> Life treads on life, and heart on heart;
> We press too close in church and mart
> To keep a dream or grave apart:

he is told. But the poem ends with

> 'Glory to God—to God!' he saith:
> KNOWLEDGE BY SUFFERING ENTERETH,
> AND LIFE IS PERFECTED BY DEATH.

In addition to the lapidary style of the last two lines, it is further flawed by the Nonconformist laundering of Shelley's

> Life, like a dome of many-coloured glass,
> Stains the white radiance of eternity.

Another group of poems with religious sentiments is of the Vanity-of-Human-Wishes type; "The Student," "Night and the Merry Man," and "Vanities" are examples. One of the few successful, genuinely religious poems is "Past and Future;" the religious feeling is profound and essential. One does not wish to suggest that E.B.B.'s religious feelings were not strong and genuine, only that her use of them is sometimes mechanical and extrinsic to the poem.

Some of the poetry, such as "To Bettine," "The Young Queen," "Cowper's Grave," is literary and topical and occasionally suffers from the usual flaws of too-bookish or too-parochial concerns. "The Cry of the Children" and "The Runaway Slave at Pilgrim's Point" are more vigorous and impassioned, dealing with child-labor and slavery, and characteristic of Mrs. Browning's concern with social and political issues.

The most successful of the early poems do not escape into the too-ready piety. "To Flush, My Dog" is both witty and moving. "Cyprus Wine" is a vigorous evocation of the authors the young Elizabeth and the much older Hugh Stuart Boyd read together, with brilliant, rapid sketches of the classical Greek poets. It is also a lively tribute to the warm câmaraderié of the two disparate scholars. "The Romance of the Swan's Nest" is a totally convincing, poignant poem of disillusion, while "A Man's Requirements" is wittily cynical. The later "Lord Walter's Wife" is a convoluted, Jamesian psychological study and a bold feminist statement.

"A Sea-Side Walk" (1844), edges its author toward what we consider the characteristic and genuine Victorian achievement, as opposed to the popular and sentimental. Beginning with

> We walked beside the sea
> After a day which perished silently
> Of its own glory—

it conveys a justified melancholy over things irretrievably lost. In mood and message and sea-side imagery it is related to the much later "Dover Beach" (1867) of Arnold, and offers no easy consolation in its concluding lines:

> For though we never spoke
> Of the gray water and the shaded rock,
> Dark wave and stone unconsciously were fused
> Into the plaintive speaking that we used
> Of absent friends and memories unforsook;
> And, had we seen each other's face, we had
>   Seen haply each was sad.

Apart from these and a few other very good poems, the first sustained, consistently fine achievement is *Sonnets from the Portuguese,* whose feelings were felt upon the pulse. Some of the earlier flaws remain here and there, but do not dominate.

While the poetry must stand on its own merits, it is undeniable that one can enjoy it more and understand it better by reading the love letters[1] with it. In these letters and poems we have a unique combination: both sides of an intimate correspondence and its distillation in poetry. Elizabeth's letters are both a conscious and sub-conscious self-revelation, in the beginning as a writer and a person keenly engaged by her own time, later as a woman, a member of an unusual family, and one who can look courageously at unpleasant and often inconvenient truths. Browning's letters are full of real and generous admiration for her art, and gradually become permeated with a fixed and utter committment to whatever relationship her circumstances and feelings allow. Because Browning's visits were more or less clandestine and brief, and because both were shy in each other's presence, they engaged, on paper, in spirited debates on literature, politics, duelling, capital punishment, and the "woman question." They do all this without cant or coquetry, affectation or the desire to impress. They do it with wit and zest, a splendid playing with words, and allusions ranging from the classics and the Bible to the latest reviews. All these gifts are put to work in trying to find the best relationship for them, and how it can be realized. This is the element the poet mines from the letters and the relationship itself, and, with considerable skill and craftsmanship, sets into the sonnet form.

Elizabeth's side of the personal element in the correspondence is dominated by two fears. She is afraid of being "a stone" in Browning's path, as she put it, and of inspiring in him pity for the invalid and worship of the poet, with the woman, flawed but genuine, lost and never brought to open-eyed judgment. No poetic device or posture, these fears had very reasonable grounds. She was a well-known, widely read and admired poet and reviewer, whose intellect, invalidism, and reclusiveness were woven into a formidable mystique. She was also thirty-nine, still emotionally drained from her brother's death five years earlier, and believed herself to be passively dying. In Browning she saw a vigorous young man of thirty-three, frequent headaches notwithstanding, writing what she called—when few did—the best poetry of the age, dancing all night, walking miles daily, and in all ways poised on the edge of every kind of success. She also saw this young man as willing and almost perversely eager to burden himself with a middle-aged invalid, against, she supposed, the wishes of both their families, all their friends, and his own best interests. The transformation of this vision of the lovers and the overcoming of these fears are the preoccupations of the *Sonnets,* which, like the letters, gradually introduce other elements. Letters and poems are of a piece and illuminate each other. What is perhaps most interesting about reading them together is the glimpse we get of the poet's method. Images from Browning's letters sometimes appear in the *Sonnets,* usually in ironic reversal of his meaning and application. Other images, words, and even whole phrases from Elizabeth's own letters also find their way into the poetry, as the notes to the *Sonnets* demonstrate.

They even conclude together, in September, 1846. Judging from the letters, Sonnet I could have been written as early as June 1845 or as late as September of that year. It is safest to assume that most of the sonnets were written in the autumn and winter of 1845-1846. There is a sharp decline of verbal echoes in the letters from March 1846, while some of the earlier themes and fears remain. Dates of letters discussed are given to set at least broad limits to the composition of individual poems, but since Elizabeth re-read Browning's letters, even this is not a very reliable guide.

Perhaps the most compelling example of how the letters illuminate the poetry comes with Sonnet V:

> I life my heavy heart up solemnly,
> As once Electra her sepulchral urn,
> And, looking in thine eyes, I overturn
> The ashes at thy feet. Behold and see
> What a great heap of grief lay hid in me,
> And how the red wild sparkles dimly burn
> Through the ashen greyness. If thy foot in scorn
> Could tread them out to darkness utterly,
> It might be well perhaps. But if instead
> Thou wait beside me for the wind to blow
> The grey dust up,. . .those laurels on thine head,
> O my belovèd, will not shield thee so,
> That none of all the fires shall scorch and shred
> The hair beneath. Stand further off then! go.

It is one of the most interesting, fully realized, and perfect poems of the sequence. The use of the Greek myth in all its suggestiveness and power is masterful and sure. The poem is free of Latinate horrors ("renunciative," "exanimate,") strained conceits, and specious supernatural intervention. It works beautifully on the obvious level with its sustained image of smouldering ashes, while functioning richly on the deeper levels of significance evoked by the suggestiveness of Electra.

Sophocles' Electra is solemn on just that one occasion, when she receives the urn she thinks contains her brother's ashes. Throughout the rest of the play she is passionately enraged, an intensity of destructive emotion hinted at in "the fires shall scorch and shred. . ." and the concluding command. The sonnet reflects Elizabeth's intense effort during August and September of 1845, to grasp her complicated family relationships and see if Browning can be integrated into them. In this poem it cannot be done without great pain; the past has overwhelmed the future, and so the poem ends with an angry warning.

Any effort to understand these feelings must take into account the fact that until she met and loved Browning, Elizabeth loved utterly and valued most her brother Edward, who had drowned five years earlier. In one sense we may say that Electra is Elizabeth defending her relationship with her dead brother against the encroachment of happiness and relative normalcy. Sophocles' Electra tells us repeatedly that all she does is wait for Orestes, and the fact that she is without husband and children is both a lament and a boast. There is a lingering sense of guilt in the letters, as if loving Browning was somehow a betrayal of Edward. On December 12, 1845, Elizabeth wrote, "You stand in between me & not merely the living who stood closest, but between me & the closer graves, . .& I reproach myself for this sometimes [. . .]" (I, 318). On December 21 it is mentioned again: "[. . .] see that I, who had my warmest affections on the other side of the grave, feel that it is otherwise with me now—quite otherwise. I did not like it at first to be so much otherwise" (I, 339).

A further complication is that Elizabeth felt somehow responsible for Edward's death because, although their father had wanted him to leave Torquay where Elizabeth was recuperating and return to London, the thought of separation from him reduced her to such wretchedness that an aunt wrote to London to say it was impossible. Edward was permitted to stay, and Elizabeth was always careful to say how grateful she was her father never reproached her for her brother's death. In the summer of 1845 Elizabeth's doctor told her that she should not risk another English winter. Mr. Moulton-Barrett, however, plainly showed his disapproval of any move to a better climate for his daughter, in the full knowlege that remaining in England might cost her her life. Browning was unable to understand this attitude and Elizabeth wrote him a long and agitated letter trying to excuse her father and explain the convoluted family relationships. She told him that her father was not evil but that his system of ruling the family was, and went on to say

> But he loves us through & through it—& *I*, for one, love *him*! & when, five years ago, I lost what I loved best in the world beyond comparison & rivalship. .far better than himself as he knew. .for everyone who knew *me* could not choose but know what was my first & chiefest affection. .when I lost *that*, . .I felt that he stood nearest to me on the closed grave. .or by the unclosing sea. .I do not know which nor could ask. And I will tell you that not only he has been kind & patient & forbearing to me through the tedious trial of this illness (far more trying to standers by than you have an idea of perhaps) but that he was generous & forbearing in that hour of bitter trial, & never reproached me as he might have done & as my own soul has not spared—never once said to me then or since,

> that if it had not been for *me,* the crown of his house wd not have fallen. He *never did.* .& he might have said it, & more—& I could have answered nothing. Nothing, except that I had paid my own price. .& that the price I paid was greater than his loss. .his!!
>
> (I, 169)

But in all her hours of intense reliving and scrutinizing of the past she might have been tempted to think that her father's lack of reproach was a *quid pro quo.* Edward, like all of his siblings, had been kept from marrying when he had wanted to, and as a disinherited son trained for nothing whatever, he could not have afforded it. On that occasion Elizabeth, the only one of the children with an income independent of their father, attempted to make over her small fortune to him but was prevented from doing so. It certainly must have occurred to her that had she been allowed to do it, he would not have died at Babbacombe Bay; both father and daughter in clinging to Edward had destroyed him. This idea is quite explicit in a remark of January 26, 1846, when Elizabeth once more tried to make Browning understand her father:

> And comparing my selfreproach to what I imagined his selfreproach must certainly be (for if *I* had loved selfishly, *he* had not been kind) I felt as if I could love & forgive him for two. .(I knowing that serene generous departed spirit, & seeming left to represent it). .
>
> (I, 422)

Against the background of this mythical dimension, the poem is a warning to Browning that if he chooses to become involved he can either destroy her by his contempt or share with her an agony not of his making, and her advice is "Stand further off then! go." Browning's reply to the long passage about Edward and their father is quoted in part in the note to Sonnet XII.

It is valuable to return to such primary sources as the letters because they help us to focus on an aspect of Mrs. Browning's work and character which is usually overlooked. We are, as William S. Peterson[2] has pointed out, still very much in the grip of the Browning myth. In the sequence we find the trembling hands and tear-stained face, but ignore the stoic of Sonnets XI and XIII, the angry, commanding speaker of Sonnet V, and the person who resents the loss of "individual life" in Sonnet VI. This particular person is rarely glimpsed in the subsequent poetry. Only in *Sonnets from the Portuguese* do we have Mrs. Browning's own intensely personal and passionately experienced feelings. After her marriage and flight to Italy she turned more and more to current social and political concerns, and advocated as well as practiced a public poetry dedicated to portraying its own age with zest and candor.

These forty-four poems are therefore the unique and considerable achievement of an intelligent, lively, dedicated poet. A few of them achieve greatness, all of them have good lines, compelling imagery, and careful workmanship. Elizabeth Barrett Browning's place as an important minor poet is secure.

While earlier biographers and critics of Mrs. Browning were nearly idolatrous, the current judgment is more temperate. Virginia Woolf marked the transition to serious critical evaluation, after the years of fame and popularity, and during the years of obscurity. She characterized the Victorian artist as "one of those rare writers who risk themselves adventurously and disinterestedly in an imaginative life. . ." However, "it cannot be doubted that the long years of seclusion had done her irreparable damage as an artist."[3] Virginia Woolf's remarks, generous in recognizing the craftsmanship and candid in acknowledging the weaknesses, marked the end of the first posthumous stage, that of apotheosis.

Gardner Taplin, Mrs. Browning's most recent and most comprehensive biographer, is perhaps a little hard on the *Sonnets*, but representative of critical opinion until very recently. Although he respects Mrs. Browning's craftsmanship as demonstrated in five of the texts—he seems unaware of the Houghton MS—he nevertheless feels that "the freshness of the 'Sonnets' has faded,. . .with all their singing angels, floods of tears, chrisms, lutes, and golden thrones, they are very much in the idiom of the period."[4] It is undeniable that there is in the *Sonnets* a good deal of the idiom of Victorian album poetry, but it is also true that there is a good deal more as well.

More recently Alethea Hayter concentrates on the poetry and devotes a short chapter to *Sonnets from the Portuguese.* She does not consider these poems Mrs. Browning's best work "because in them she is dealing with an emotion too new and powerful for her to transmute it into universally valid terms. Psychologically. . .they are absorbing, but poetically the utmost poignancy of happy love is not there, as the poignancy of unhappy love is in 'Modern Love'."[5] Generally a perceptive critic, Hayter here loses the focus of her criticism. Mrs. Browning did not intend to and could not portray in this sequence "the utmost poignancy of happy love." The *Sonnets* record a struggle with and ultimate, hard-won victory over despair, self-doubt, and fear. The struggle is only clearly over in the very last poem.

Hayter gets closer to the flaw when she remarks that the imagery comes too often from that room at 50 Wimpole Street: fire, flickering and bright; pale, trembling hands; rich materials; cups of wine. But here the author is merely agreeing with Mrs. Browning herself who knew very well what her mode of life cost her as a poet. That setting included invalidism, opium-taking, a highly-colored, sometimes morbid imagination, wide, varied, sometimes feverish reading. This book, published in 1962, marks a new period in academic criticism of E.B.B. It points out Mrs. Browning's weaknesses, but not condescendingly or patronizingly, and, above all, it takes the poet seriously as a mind and creative force in the Victorian Age. In its careful, scholarly investigation of Mrs. Browning's sources, it documents fully Mrs. Woolf's earlier brilliant, impressionistic judgment.

Indeed, there are several points at which the critiques of Woolf, Taplin, and Hayter converge. Woolf and Hayter see Mrs. Browning's mind and reactions as irredeemably circumscribed by her isolation, and forced into channels alien to themselves. Taplin and Hayter criticize the dated and idiosyncratic imagery with which she sometimes expressed her perceptions. They all admire the person, the unstinting nature of her effort, the integrity of her craftsmanship. Hayter, to be sure, in a discussion of the technical aspects of the sonnet sequence, discerns "the straining muscles and suffused countenance of the prisoner in the strait-jacket." She demonstrates that while Mrs. Browning thought she was conforming entirely to her Italian model, she in fact disregarded the required division of statement; even so, "the final lines of her sonnets have. . .impressive unaffected excellence."[6] It is difficult to imagine how serious critical judgment might depart radically from these views.

There is currently a good deal of interest in Mrs. Browning, some of it due to the growing interest in women writers generally. Most critics of this type have resisted the temptation to preempt Mrs. Browning for any feminist causes, a role she could not fit without some distortion. She is certainly being taken much more seriously now than she has been throughout most of this century. William S. Peterson, editor of the British Library Manuscript facsimile mentioned earlier, focuses on the mind instead of the myth, and examines Mrs. Browning's poetic theory. He investigates her relationship to her great contemporaries and her predecessors, notably Shelley, among the Romantics, as well as demonstrating the originality of her work. Julia Markus, in a fine edition of *Casa Guidi Windows*,[7] makes a strong case for Mrs. Browning as the poet of the Italian *Risorgimento*. Cora Kaplan's introduction to a recent reprint of *Aurora Leigh*[8] discusses the sources of Mrs. Browning's ideas, and how she modified them in her art and social theory. The lyricist in Mrs. Browning continues to be read, while the polemicist is being widely studied. Like everyone else, Mrs. Browning has been subjected to the academic oscillation between exploitation and neglect, and varying fashions and trends in criticism. All throughout this period, however, one could find, wherever books are sold, editions of *Sonnets from the Portuguese,* poems which have never ceased to sing to some part of the reading public.

NOTES

[1] Only a very few citations are from letters to other correspondents, and these are identified with conventional footnotes. The bulk of references to letters comes from the standard edition of Elvan Kintner, *The Letters of Robert Browning and Elizabeth Barrett Barrett 1845-1846* (Cambridge: The Belknap Press of Harvard University Press, 1969), 2 Vols. These references are identified by date either before or after the quotation, and always by volume and page number immediately after each quotation.

[2] Elizabeth Barrett Browning, *Sonnets from the Portuguese,* ed. William S. Peterson (Barre: Barre Publishing, 1977). This is a handsome facsimile edition of the British Library Manuscript, with an interesting and valuable introduction.

[3] Virginia Woolf, *The Common Reader,* Series Two (1932: rpt. New York: Harcourt, Brace and Company, 1948), pp. 224-25.

[4] Gardner Taplin, *The Life of Elizabeth Barrett Browning* (New Haven: Yale University Press, 1957), p. 236.

[5] Alethea Hayter, *Mrs. Browning: A Poet's Work and Its Setting* (London: Faber and Faber, 1962), p. 103.

[6] Hayter, p. 107.

[7] Elizabeth Barrett Browning, *Casa Guidi Windows,* ed. Julia Markus (New York: The Browning Institute, Inc., 1977).

[8] Elizabeth Barrett Browning, *Aurora Leigh and Other Poems,* introduced by Cora Kaplan (London: The Women's Press, Ltd., 1978).

TEXTUAL INTRODUCTION

Composition and Publishing History

On January 10, 1845, Robert Browning wrote a letter to Elizabeth Barrett Barrett. He wrote to a poet already widely read and to a woman known to be erudite, reclusive, and plagued by a wasting illness which he thought was a permanent and crippling injury of the spine. It was a young man's letter, these first words to a stranger, spontaneous, generous, and affectionate. An uncharacteristic act for the usually reticent Browning, it brought extraordinary results. He had just read her *Poems, 1844*, before he wrote "I do [. . .] love these books with all my heart—and I love you too [. . .]." Reluctant as she normally was to encourage new correspondences and relationships, Elizabeth was not impervious to these words. She had read and admired Browning's work and even had a picture of him in her room. That the praise and warmth of Browning's letter gave her great joy is evident in her immediate and spirited reply. It is also evident in the exulting tone with which she reported to other correspondents that she had had a letter from Browning, "poet and mystic."

There were to be many letters between the two poets, 573 in all, in the months to follow. Elizabeth, however, wrote not only the letters; she also responded with the poetry for which she is best known today. The *Sonnets from the Portuguese* were written during the twenty-month correspondence and courtship which they chronicle.

Although Elizabeth began writing the sonnet sequence between June and September 1845, and finished it by September 1846, Browning did not see it until 1849, while they were summering at Bagni di Lucca. We have his own word for this date and place in a letter Browning wrote to Leigh Hunt while the Browning's were again staying at Bagni di Lucca in 1957:

> I should like to tell you that I never suspected the existence of those *Sonnets from the Portuguese* till three years after they were written: they were shown to me at this very place eight years ago, in consequence to some words of mine, just as they had been suppressed thro' some mistaken word: it was I who would not bear that sacrifice and thought of the subterfuge of a name.[1]

Elizabeth was still alive at the time this letter was written and had he had any doubts, Browning would surely have consulted her. It should also be noted that while they did not normally read each other's letters to other people, Elizabeth may well have read this one since she added a full-length letter of her own at the end of Robert's.

In 1864 Browning wrote to a friend, Julia Wedgwood, about first seeing the sonnets, but in greater detail. He did not mention specific dates but spoke of "all this dealy," between the time of composition and his seeing the poetry, resulting from a remark of his. He also told Miss Wedgwood that he could still see the window, at Lucca, at which he was standing when Elizabeth gave him the poems, "with the tall mimosa in front, and the little church-court to the right."[2] In 1881 the story was repeated to Peter Bayne, to whom Browning wrote that Elizabeth had given him the poetry at "Bagni di Lucca, after the birth of her child, a few months before."[3] As we shall see below, it is of considerable importance to establish both the year and the place of Browning's seeing the sonnet sequence for the first time.

Browning also tells us how the reading public came to see the *Sonnets*. In the letter to Hunt cited earlier he makes it clear that he would not sacrifice the sequence to his need for privacy. It was he who insisted on publication, and he who "thought of the subterfuge of a name." This "name," *Sonnets from the Portuguese*, was intended to suggest a translation. Another tactic was to move Sonnet XLII to another part of *Poems*, 1850, since it was obviously autobiographical in its link to an earlier published poem of Elizabeth's.

The *Sonnets* were published for the first time in the second

Textual Introduction xxi

edition of Mrs. Browning's *Poems* in 1850. They appeared again, with revisions, in *Poems, 1853,* and once more, extensively revised, in *Poems, 1856.* No separate edition of *Sonnets from the Portuguese* appeared in Mrs. Browning's lifetime.

This simple and straightforward publishing history of the sonnet sequence was unchallenged until shortly after Browning's death in 1889, and it has been generally acknowledged since 1934. But between 1890 and 1934 it was confused and distorted by a most extraordinary literary hoax. At some time in 1893 copies of an octavo volume of forty-seven pages of foolscap appeared among the collectors and bibliophiles of London, with the title

SONNETS

BY

E.B.B.

READING:

[NOT FOR PUBLICATION] [4]

1847

The volume contained the same forty-three *Sonnets from the Portuguese* as the genuine first edition in *Poems, 1850,* in the same sequence. Differences between the alleged first edition and the genuine one are minor and are probably printer's errors. From the time of its appearance in 1893 until 1934, this edition, known as the Reading Sonnets, was generally believed to be the genuine first edition of Mrs. Browning's sonnet sequence. Individual collectors, booksellers, and institutions in England and the United States paid large sums for copies of this forgery. In July 1934 a book with the unsensational title *An Enquiry into the Nature of Certain Nineteenth Century Pamphlets* appeared, and its revelations made front-page news in English dailies. The authors, John Carter and Graham Pollard, proclaimed the Reading Sonnets a forgery and provided incontrovertible scientific proof. By means of chemical tests and analyses, Carter and Pollard discovered that the paper on which the Reading Sonnets was printed could not have been manufactured before 1874. A close study of nineteenth-century type revealed that certain letters of the type used in the Reading pamphlet were not cut for the printer until after 1880.[5]

While the exposure of the Reading Sonnets was the most spectacular achievement of *An Enquiry,* the book also proved spurious many other allegedly rare nineteenth-century works. The authors did not make any specific accusations; however, it was obvious that the over fifty items they discussed had one thing in common. What drew these pamphlets together under one roof was that each had some connection with Thomas J. Wise, gentleman, essayist, bibliographer of international repute, and owner of one of the most notable private collections of his time, the Ashley Library. The implicit identity of the forger was as shocking as the forgery. Discussions of Wise's activity have filled volumes since 1934, and the controversy over who were accomplices and who were dupes rages on.

Such peripheral questions remain, but Wise and the Reading Sonnets are discredited. Unfortunately, reprints of the spurious publishing history in earlier editions continue to appear and mislead the reader. The Cambridge edition of Mrs. Browning's *Poetical Works,* for example, reprinted in 1974, lamentably announces the Reading Sonnets as the first edition of *Sonnets from the Portuguese.*

Editorial Principles

For a variorum edition of *Sonnets from the Portuguese* there are six texts in all. Three of these are manuscripts, and three are editions published in Mrs. Browning's lifetime, in 1850, 1853, and 1856 as part of her *Poems.* The first edition of *Poems* was published in 1844; *Sonnets* appeared in print for the first time in the second edition of *Poems* (1850).

The earliest extant manuscript version, the Morgan Library manuscript, is incomplete, ending with Sonnet XXIX; Sonnets

Textual Introduction xxiii

XVII and XVIII are missing. Each poem is on the recto of a separate sheet of white paper, 110 x 161 mm., mounted on larger sheets. The ink is faded brown with corrections in a darker brown as well as in a very dark, almost black ink. The MS is bound with an 1853 silhouette of Mrs. Browning by Turner, which has never been engraved.

The next version is the British Library manuscript, the most important in its associations. It seems to be the version Mrs. Browning gave to her husband and the one he kept until his death when it went to their son. It contains all forty-four sonnets and has a date at the end:

50 Wimpole St.
1846, Sept.

A second entry, under the first:

Married—September 12th,
1846

is in the same darker ink used for most of the revisions in this MS, and is similar to the darker of the two in the Morgan MS. The paper, once either pale blue or pale green, is now almost white and measures 115 x 180 mm. This second manuscript includes the sonnet beginning "My future will not copy fair my past" as XVII (missing from the Morgan manuscript altogether).

The same XVII in the British Library manuscript is absent from the third version, the Houghton manuscript, which is consecutively numbered from one to forty-three. The Houghton MS was the printer's copy for the 1850 edition; it has compositors' names, it lacks Mrs. Browning's customary & for *and,* and is in general a carefully prepared copy. The paper is pale blue, 110 x 161 mm.

The fourth text, in the second edition of *Poems* (1850), follows the Houghton MS in excluding what was XVII in the British Library version from the sonnet sequence but has the poem elsewhere in the collection, a practice which was continued in the 1853 edition as well. In 1856 the sonnet was restored to the sequence as XLII while the fomer XLII and XLIII became XLIII and XLIV.

On the evidence now available, the copy-text for a variorum edition of *Sonnets from the Portuguese* is clearly the last edition of the author's lifetime, that of 1856. We know from the letters of both Elizabeth and Robert Browning that Mrs. Browning worked very hard on revisions of each successive edition and that they considered all changes important, including punctuation. Her method for the 1850 edition was to enter revisions into a copy of the 1844 edition—a part of this volume is at Wellesley—while the new poems, including *Sonnets from the Portuguese*, were sent in MS. Browning asked Edward Chapman to send the proofs to his sister, Sarianna Browning, and Elizabeth wrote to Sarianna apologizing for the condition of the text. It is clear that Miss Browning was not authorized to make any changes and what she had to do was see to it that the proofs reflected the printer's copy faithfully. This arrangement clearly eliminates any possibility of authorial changes at the proof stage. It also means that the person checking proof and printer's copy against each other, presumably Miss Browning,[6] might have made mistakes in deciphering Mrs. Browning's handwriting. There are forty-five changes from the printer's copy—the Houghton MS—in the 1850 edition, when there ought to have been none. These changes are all in the area of accidentals, according to Greg's classic definition.[7] On the face of it this situation would argue for a composite copy-text reflecting substantive changes up to and including the 1856 edition while retaining the accidentals of the printer's copy for the 1850 edition, the Houghton MS. However, I do not believe such a procedure is justified in view of the nature of the forty-five changes, Browning's specific mention of changes in punctuation for the 1853 edition, and Mrs. Browning's preparation of the 1856 edition.

The forty-five presumably unauthorized revisions of accidentals which appeared in 1850 are tabulated in the Appendix. It is obvious that the majority of them are unimportant impositions of house-style, such as double for single quotation marks and hyphenation. Another group of revisions is restored to the Houghton reading in subsequent editions, leaving one-third of the revised accidentals unchanged. Considering the fact that Mrs. Browning revised again in 1853 and 1856, any tinkering with the 1856 edition of *Sonnets* on behalf of those original unauthorized revisions is not justified.

The second reason for choosing the 1856 edition as the copy-text has to do with the Brownings' attitude toward punctuation. It is clear from the correspondence with Chapman preceding the 1853 edition that they placed considerable importance on any changes in it. We have neither printer's copy nor proofs (this time the proofs were read by Elizabeth's sister, Arabel Barrett), but we know that even though Mrs. Browning's revisions were mostly in punctuation, the Brownings considered the changes weighty enough to justify a note to the reader. Since we have no way of ascertaining which changes are due to the printer and which to the author, it is too risky to stop with the accidentals of the Houghton MS.

Finally, since we know that Mrs. Browning revised again for the 1856 edition and on that occasion read the proofs herself—when most of the changes of 1853 were retained and many more added—the 1856 edition, *in toto,* is clearly the copy-text.

Related to the question of text is the problem of authorial control. Proofs are the only incontrovertible evidence for establishing the degree of an author's control, and we do not have them for *Sonnets from the Portuguese.* In any case, the Brownings checked proofs for the 1856 edition only, because they were then in France and in England. During the preparation and publication of the 1850 and 1853 editions they had been in Italy, and it would have been too time-consuming and expensive to receive and read the proofs there. What we do have, however, is an extensive correspondence from both the Brownings to their friends and Edward Chapman, Elizabeth's publisher.

Letters to various correspondents show that Mrs. Browning worked hard and long on revisions. The second edition of *Poems,* that of 1850, occupied her for at least five months. She revised again for the third edition in 1853 when Browning wrote several letters to Chapman on her behalf. In a letter of March 5, 1853, Browning wrote the publisher that since the alterations for the new edition are "few and trifling. . .changes in punctuation for the most part," no proofs would be necessary. When he reached the end of the letter, however, he had second thoughts and wrote "as there *are* alterations" it would be "safer to send the proofs to Miss Barrett" (Elizabeth's sister Arabel), unless Chapman and Hall had someone on whom they could "altogether depend."[8]

Five weeks later Elizabeth was still revising, and in another letter to Chapman Browning thought the changes were numerous enough to justify a postscript to the advertisement.[9] The postscript reads

> In the present edition the author has done her best to remedy the oversights and defects of that former revision, which her absence from England rendered less complete than it should have been.
>
> Florence, 1853[10]

The Brownings' insistence on control over the text is particularly evident during the preparation of the 1856 edition, when Robert wrote Edward Chapman that "we *must* see the proofs."[11]

Taken together, the correspondence indicates that Mrs. Browning revised for each edition, and that the Brownings wanted to exercise more and more control over the text. Lacking proofs we cannot assert that they achieved absolute control, but we can assume that they had a good deal of it, especially over the 1856 edition. There can be no doubt that the version of *Sonnets from the Portuguese* contained in that last edition of *Poems* in Mrs. Browning's lifetime is the one she intended us to read above all others.

NOTES

[1] Thurman L. Hood, ed., *Letters of Robert Browning Collected by Thomas J. Wise* (London: John Murray, 1933), p. 48. It is generally believed that the "mistaken word" alluded to was a remark critical of self-revelation in poetry. In 1849, however, he seems to have expressed a different view, prompting E.B.B. to show him what she had done in that line.

[2] Richard Curle, ed., *Robert Browning and Julia Wedgwood* (New York: Fredrick A. Stokes, 1937), pp. 99-100.

[3] John Carter, "Correspondence," *Times Literary Supplement*, November 15, 1934, p. 795. Pen Browning was born on March 9, 1849.

[4] The brackets are not mine.

[5] John Carter and Graham Pollard, *An Enquiry into the Nature of Certain Nineteenth Century Pamphlets* (1934; rpt. New York: Haskell House, 1971), p. 167.

[6] There is some evidence that John Forster too was involved, but it is impossible to ascertain in what capacity. On July 29, 1850, Browning wrote to John Kenyon that Forster "is always most kind, and just now, among his multifarious occupations, is caring for Ba's new Edition." (Hood, p. 30.)
While it is difficult to imagine Sarianna Browning taking liberties with Mrs. Browning's text, it is not quite so preposterous to think of Forster doing so.

[7] W. W. Greg, "The Rationale of Copy Text," (1950) *Bibliography and Textual Criticism*, ed. O. M. Brack, Jr., and Warner Barnes (Chicago: The University of Chicago Press, 1969), p. 43.

[8] William C. De Vane and Kenneth L. Knickerbocker, eds., *New Letters of Robert Browning* (New Haven: Yale University Press, 1950), pp, 58-59.

[9]*New Letters*, pp. 62-63.

[10]Elizabeth Barrett Browning, *Poems*, 3rd ed. (London: Chapman and Hall, 1853), II, viii.

[11]*New Letters*, p. 92.

LIST OF ABBREVIATIONS AND SYMBOLS

M   Earliest extant MS of *Sonnets from the Portuguese,* now at the Pierpont Morgan Library.

B   Second MS of the *Sonnets,* and the one which Mrs. Browning gave her husband in 1849. This MS is now in the British Library.

H   The final MS version of the *Sonnets,* prepared by Mrs. Browning for inclusion in *Poems,* 1850. This MS is now in the private collection of Mr. Arthur Houghton, Jr.

(R)   Fannie Ratchford's reading of a heavily scored out word or line. While I examined all three of the MSS I do not think I could have arrived at these readings without Miss Rachford's having suggested them.

[...]   Both Brownings used ellipses in their correspondence, and Mrs. Browning used them liberally in her poetry. To avoid confusion between their ellipses and mine, which are always used in the conventional way to indicate a break in the text, I have put mine in brackets.

Kintner   *The Letters of Robert Browning and Elizabeth Barrett Barrett 1845-1846.* Ed. Elvan Kintner. Cambridge: The Belknap Press of Harvard University Press, 1969.

Porter and Clarke   *The Complete Works of Elizabeth Barrett Browning.* Eds. Charlotte Porter and Helen Clarke. 6 vols. 1900; rpt. New York: AMS

Press Inc., 1973. All citations are from volume 3.

Sonnets from the Portuguese

I

1 I thought once how Theocritus had sung
2 Of the sweet years, the dear and wished for years,
3 Who each one in a gracious hand appears
4 To bear a gift for mortals, old or young:
5 And, as I mused it in his antique tongue,
6 I saw, in gradual vision through my tears,
7 The sweet, sad years, the melancholy years,
8 Those of my own life, who by turns had flung
9 A shadow across me. Straightway I was 'ware,
10 So weeping, how a mystic Shape did move
11 Behind me, and drew me backward by the hair,
12 And a voice said in mastery while I strove, . .
13 'Guess now who holds thee?'—'Death,' I said. But there,
14 The silver answer rang . . 'Not Death, but Love.'

1 Theocritus (fl. c. 270 B.C.), some of whose work E.B.B. had translated, was a Greek poet known for his *Idylls* and as the founder of pastoral poetry. (*The Oxford Companion to Classical Literature*, 1937). The "antique tongue" is Greek. Porter and Clarke trace this allusion to Idyll XV. While Mrs. Browning would have read Theocritus in the original, here are the lines as translated by Francis Fawkes (1810):

> Once more the soft-foot Hours approaching slow,
> Restore Adonis from the realms below;
> Welcome to man they come with silent pace,
> Diffusing benisons to human race.

11 Porter and Clarke point out that in Book I of the *Iliad* the unseen

Athene drew Achilles backward by the hair.

Heading

M: *Sonnets.*

   Death or Love. with *or* written over &

B: *Sonnet I*

   Thoughts in or *on passing* written over *Death or Love* and both cancelled (R)

   3 in upper right

H: *Sonnets from the Portuguese*

   Death or Love—cancelled

   I

   The compositor's name, *Richardson,* written at upper left

2   M: *& wished for* written above cancelled word, possibly *cherished*

4   M: *mortals* for *mortals,*

5   B: *And* for *And,*

6   M: Originally *I saw in vision through my sadden tears,* with *gradual* inserted before *vision*

   sadden cancelled

   B: *saw* for *saw,*

7   M: *sweet* for *sweet,*

   B: *years, . .* for second *years,*

   H: As in B

   1850:   As in B

7	1853:	As in B
8	M:	*life* for *life,*
9	M:	*'across* for *across*
		me! for *me.*
11	M:	*me'* for first *me,*
		& for *and*
		hair: for *hair,*
	B:	*me* for first *me,*
		hair; for *hair,*
	H:	*hair;* for *hair,*
	1850:	As in H
	1853:	As in H
12	M:	*And a voice cried aloud, the while I strove,*
	B:	*And a voice cried in mastery, while I strove,*
13	M:	*"Guess now, who holds thee?" "Death," I said! but there,*
	B:	*'Guess now who holds thee!'—'Death,' I said!: but, there,*
	H:	*'Guess now who holds thee!'.. 'Death'! I said. But, there,*
	1850:	*"Guess now who holds thee?"—"Death!" I said. But there,*
	1853:	As in 1850 but with single quotation marks
14	M:	Double instead of single quotation marks
	1850:	As in M

II

1 But only three in all God's universe
2 Have heard this word thou hast said,—Himself beside
3 Thee speaking, and me listening! and replied
4 One of us .. *that* was God, .. and laid the curse
5 So darkly on my eyelids, as to amerce
6 My sight from seeing thee,—that if I had died,
7 The deathweights, placed there, would have signified
8 Less absolute exclusion. 'Nay' is worse
9 From God than from all others, O my friend!
10 Men could not part us with their worldly jars,
11 Nor the seas change us, nor the tempests bend;
12 Our hands would touch for all the mountain-bars,—
13 And, heaven being rolled between us at the end,
14 We should but vow the faster for the stars.

---

5   *amerce*—F. amercier. To fine arbitrarily, to punish. "To be amerced for sins unknown," Byron, *Cain,* III, i. mulct, deprive of. Dr. Johnson defines the word as meaning "To punish with a pecuniary penalty; to exact a fine; to inflict a forfeiture."

7   *deathweights*—coins were used for these, down to the late 19th century. The vestigial pagan idea that the dead needed money coincided with the convenient size, shape and weight of coins.

9   In September 1845 Browning declared his love once more and on September 16 Elizabeth wrote: "But something worse than even a sense of unworthiness, GOD, has put between us!" (I, 195).

6 *Sonnets from the Portuguese*

Heading

M: *Sonnets. II*

     Love's obstacles

B: *Sonnet II*

     Obstacles cancelled

     4 in upper right

H: *Sonnets from the Portuguese*

     II

1   M: *three,* for *three*

         universe, for *universe*

2   M: *thou'* for *thou*

         said;— for *said,—*

    H: *said;* for *said,—*

    1950:   As in H

    1853:   As in H

3   M: *&* for first *and*

         And for second *and*

    B: As in M

         speaking for *speaking,*

         listening: for *listening,—*

    H: *speaking* for *speaking,*

    1850:   As in H

    1853:   As in H

A Variorum Edition 7

4   M: *One of us,— that was God! & laid the curse*

       B: *One of us . . that was God! . . and laid the curse*

       H: As in B

       1850:   As in B

       1853:   As in B

5   M: Apostrophe between *to* and *amerce*

       B: *eyelids* for *eyelids,*

       H: As in B

       1850:   As in B

       1853:   As in B

6   M: *The sight of thee from me, . .*

            My sight from thy sight written above and changed to *My sight from seeing thee, . .*

       B: *thee; . .* for *thee,—*

7   M: *death-weights,* for *deathweights,*

8   M: *exclusion!* for *exclusion.*

       1850:   *"Nay"* for *'Nay'*

9   M: *dearest friend!* with *dearest* cancelled

            O my written above cancelled word.

10   M: Heavily cancelled first words. The line may have begun *They our loves*. *Seas* written over *They*, and *His* over *Seas*. The whole phrase was then cancelled for *O that men* written above the line.

            O that cancelled and *men* changed to *Men*.

            Worldly inserted between *their* and *jar* and *s* added to *jar*

            Men could not part us with their worldly jars, . .

       B: *jars,—* for *jars,*

11	M:	*tempests,* for *tempests*
		bend! for *bend;*
	B:	*seas,* for *seas*
	B:	The rest as in M
	H:	*bend:* for *bend;*
	1850:	As in H
	1853:	As in H
12	M:	*Our hands would touch above the mountain-bars,*
		Hearts written above the line and cancelled
		Our and *would* cancelled and restored
		S added to *bar*
	B:	*touch,* for *touch*
		bars: for *bars,—*
	H:	*touch,* for *touch*
		bars;— for *bars,—*
	1850:	As in H
13	M:	*And Heaven being rolled between us, at the end,*
	B:	*And heaven being rolled between us, at the end,*
14	B:	*faster,* for *faster*

III

1 Unlike are we, unlike, O princely Heart!
2 Unlike our uses and our destinies.
3 Our ministering two angels look surprise
4 On one another, as they strike athwart
5 Their wings in passing. Thou, bethink thee, art
6 A guest for queens to social pageantries,
7 With gages from a hundred brighter eyes
8 Than tears even can make mine, to ply thy part
9 Of chief musician. What hast *thou* to do
10 With looking from the lattice-lights at me,
11 A poor, tired, wandering singer, . . singing through
12 The dark, and leaning up a cypress tree?
13 The chrism is on thine head,—on mine, the dew,—
14 And Death must dig the level where these agree.

7 *gages*—something deposited to ensure the performance of some action, and liable to forfeiture in case of non-performance. Dr. Johnson defines it as "a pledge; a pawn; a caution; anything given in security."

to gage—fix or fasten in or upon

10 *lattice-lights*—Although *lattice* can mean one of the divisions of the auditorium of a theatre, here it most likely means the latticed window of a brightly-lit room. The image in lines 9-12 expresses E.B.B.'s frequent ironic reversal of Browning's idea of their relationship. He just missed meeting her years earlier and felt, he wrote in his first letter, he'd passed close by "some world's-wonder in chapel or crypt" (I, 3-4). Three months later, before they had met, he wrote he had been near Wimpole Street but hadn't dared to enter it and look at her

house.

13 *chrism*—oil of anointing used in the administration of certain sacraments in the Eastern and Western Church, and in coronation. Cf. Sonnet XXXVIII in which the second kiss, on hair and forehead, is the "chrism of love."

dew—of what E.B.B. calls the "grave-damps" in Sonnet XXIII.

Heading

M: *Sonnets. III*

B: *Sonnet III*

   King's courting cancelled (R)

   5 in upper right

H: *Sonnets from the Portuguese*

   III

1 M: *unlike* for *unlike,*

2 M: *&* for *and*

           destinies! for *destinies.*

   B: *destinies!* for *destinies.*

   H: *uses,* for *uses*

   1850: As in H

           destinies . . for *destinies.*

4 M: *another* for *another,*

6 M: *A guest for queens to masques & pageantries,—*

7 M: *thousand* for *hundred*

8 M: *Than even my tears make mine, to ply thy part*

A Variorum Edition 11

8   B: *tears,* for *tears*

            even, for *even*

    H: As in B

    1850:   As in B

9   B: *musician!* for *musician.*

            do, for *do*

10 B: *me* for *me,*

11 M: *A poor tired wandering singer, singing through*

            question mark after singer cancelled and replaced with a comma

    B: *singer?* . . for *singer,* . .

    H: As in B

    1850:   As in B

    1853:   As in B

12 M: *The dark, and leaning up a cypress-tree?*

            leant against changed to *leaning 'gainst*

            'gainst cancelled for a word, cancelled above the line and *up* inserted

    B: As final reading of M

13 M: *dew,* . . for *dew,—*

IV

1 Thou has thy calling to some palace-floor,

2 Most gracious singer of high poems! where

3 The dancers will break footing, from the care

4 Of watching up thy pregnant lips for more.

5 And dost thou lift this house's latch too poor

6 For hand of thine? and canst thou think and bear

7 To let thy music drop here unaware

8 In folds of golden fulness at my door?

9 Look up and see the casement broken in,

10 The bats and owlets builders in the roof!

11 My cricket chirps against thy mandolin.

12 Hush, call no echo up in further proof

13 Of desolation! there's a voice within

14 That weeps . . as thou must sing . . alone, aloof.

Sonnet IV restates III, and both introduce a frequent theme in the sequence, the contrast between his richness and her poverty. Later the sense of inappropriateness is less intense, no longer a source of pain because to some extent her love and, above all, his love for her, raise her to worthiness. Her cheeks are pale, faded (VIII, XI), she is like a worn viol (XXXII) whom any other musician would cast down angrily, she is a poor, tired, wandering singer leading a weary minstrel life (III, XI), she is a wet-winged dove (XXXV), her place is at the prison-wall (XLI, VIII), her life is in ashes and she will not touch his purple and fine crystal with her dust and poison (V, IX). He, on the other hand, is a liberal and princely giver (VIII) with princely Heart (III), he is noble and like a king, a guest for queens (XVI, III), he is the most gracious singer of high poems in palaces (IV), and a dove-like help (XXXI). The symbols for him and his gifts are laurel, gold and purple.

Heading

M: *Sonnets. IV*

B: *Sonnet IV*

　　 6 in upper right

H: *Sonnets from the Portuguese*

　　 IV

1　B: *palace floor,* for *palace-floor,*

　　H: As in B

　　1850:   As in B

　　1853:   As in B

2　M: *poems!,* for *poems!*

　　B: *poems, ..* for *poems!*

3　M: *footing* for *footing,*

　　B: As in M

　　1850:   As in M

　　1853:   As in M

4　M: *Of watching up thy silent lips for more!*

5　B: *latch,* for *latch*

6　M: & for second *and*

　　B: As in M

7　M: *unaware,* for *unaware*

9　M: *Look up and see the lattice broken in—*

　　B: *Look up, & see the casement broken in—*

10	M:	& for *and*
		owlets, for *owlets*
	B:	& for *and*
		roof: for *roof!*
11	M:	*mandolin!* for *mandolin.*
	B:	As in M
12	M:	*Hush!* for *Hush,*
	B:	As in M
	H:	As in M
	1850:	As in M
	1853:	As in M
13	M:	*within,* for *within*
14	M:	*That weeps . . as thou must henceforth sing . . <u>aloof!</u>*
	B:	*That weeps . . as thou must sing . . alone, . . aloof!*
	H:	*That* written over another word

V

1 I lift my heavy heart up solemnly,

2 As once Electra her sepulchral urn,

3 And, looking in thine eyes, I overturn

4 The ashes at thy feet. Behold and see

5 What a great heap of grief lay hid in me,

6 And how the red wild sparkles dimly burn

7 Through the ashen greyness. If thy foot in scorn

8 Could tread them out to darkness utterly,

9 It might be well perhaps. But if instead

10 Thou wait beside me for the wind to blow

11 The grey dust up, . . . those laurels on thine head,

12 O my belovèd, will not shield thee so,

13 That none of all the fires shall scorch and shred

14 The hair beneath. Stand further off then! go.

3   Sophocles' Electra receives her brother's ashes with solemnity and despair, only to learn that he is alive and beside her. Orestes returned after years of exile to help Electra avenge their father's murder by their mother, Clytemnestra, and her lover, Aegisthus. This sonnet with its mythical overtones is an important portrayal of E.B.B.'s early efforts to integrate Browning into her complex personal relationships with her family.

11-12   This image was probably suggested by Browning's phrase in a letter of August 21, 1845: "since thunder frightens you, for all the laurels,—". (I, 165). Kintner's note points to Sonnet V, and tells us that Pliny, in *Natural History XV,* says that lightning does not strike laurel. Tiberius used to wear a wreath of it during storms.

18   *Sonnets from the Portuguese*

There is a detailed discussion of Sonnet V in the Critical Introduction.

Heading

M: *Sonnets. V*

B: *Sonnet V*

     7 in upper right

H: *Sonnets from the Portuguese*

     V

2   M: *urn—* for *urn,*

3   M: *And* for *And,*

4   M: *&* for *and*

     B: As in M

5   M: *me,—* for *me,*

7   M: *greyness!* for *greyness.*

          grey ashes. written above *ashen greyness!* with nothing cancelled

8   M: *Could* written over *Should*

9   M: *perhaps!* for *perhaps.*

11   M: *The grey dust up, ... those laurels on thy head,*

     B: *up, ...* for *up, . . .*

     H: *head* for *head,*

12   M: *so* for *so,*

     B: *belovèd* for *belovèd*

     H: As in B

A Variorum Edition

12   1850:   As in B

       1850:   *My* for *my*

       1853:   As in B

13   M: & for *and*

       B: As in M

14   M: *Thy copious locks! Stand farther off then! Go!*

       B: *Thy copious locks!* cancelled (R)

               The hair beneath! written above

               Go. for *go.*

       H: *The hair beneath. Stand further off then! Go.*

       1850:   As in H

       1853:   As in H

VI

1 Go from me. Yet I feel that I shall stand
2 Henceforward in thy shadow. Nevermore
3 Alone upon the threshold of my door
4 Of individual life, I shall command
5 The uses of my soul, nor lift my hand
6 Serenely in the sunshine as before,
7 Without the sense of that which I forbore, ..
8 Thy touch upon the palm. The widest land
9 Doom takes to part us, leaves thy heart in mine
10 With pulses that beat double. What I do
11 And what I dream include thee, as the wine
12 Must taste of its own grapes. And when I sue
13 God for myself, He hears that name of thine,
14 And sees within my eyes, the tears of two.

12-13   "Think of your very own, who bids God bless you when she prays for herself!—" January 13, 1846. (I, 386.) The poem was almost certainly written before this date.

Heading

M: *Sonnets. VI*

B: *Sonnet VI*

22   *Sonnets from the Portuguese*

B: *8* in upper right

H: *Sonnets from the Portuguese*

      A lover in absence cancelled

      VI

1   M: *me!* for *me.*

2   M: *shadow!* for *shadow.*

5   M: *soul,—* for *soul,*

6   M: *Up whitely in the sunshine as before,..*

7   M: *forbore..* for *forbore,..*

     B: *forbore,...* for *forbore,..*

     H: As in B

8   M: *Thy touch upon the palm! The widest land,*

9   M: *thy* written over *thine*

10   M: *double!* for *double.*

12   M: *grapes!* for *grapes.*

13   M: *thine,..* for *thine,*

14   M: *eyes* for *eyes,*

          two underlined

VII

1 The face of all the world is changed, I think,
2 Since first I heard the footsteps of thy soul
3 Move still, oh, still, beside me, as they stole
4 Betwixt me and the dreadful outer brink
5 Of obvious death, where I, who thought to sink,
6 Was caught up into love, and taught the whole
7 Of life in a new rhythm. The cup of dole
8 God gave for baptism, I am fain to drink,
9 And praise its sweetness, Sweet, with the anear.
10 The names of country, heaven, are changed away
11 For where thou art or shalt be, there or here;
12 And this . . this lute and song . . loved yesterday,
13 (The singing angels know) are only dear,
14 Because thy name moves right in what they say.

7-9   These lines recall the sonnet "Past and Future," written before E.B.B. knew Browning.

Heading

M: *Sonnets. VII*

   Love's new creation

   changes between *Love's* and *new* cancelled

B: *Sonnet VII*

     9 in upper right

H: *Sonnets from the Portuguese*

     VII

1   M: *The face of all the world is changed I think*

     B: As in M

3   M: *Move still . . oh, still . . beside me—as they stole*

     B: *Move still . . oh still . . beside me: as they stole*

     H: *beside me;* for *beside me,*

     1850:   As in H

4   B: *&* for *and*

5   M: *death, . .* for *death,*

     B: As in M

          I for *I,*

          sink for *sink,*

     H: *Of obvious death, where I who thought to sink*

          1850:   As in H

          1853:   As in H

6   M: *love* for *love,*

          & for *and*

     B: As in M

     H: *love* for *love,*

          1850:   As in H

          1853:   As in H

9	M:	*the* for *its*
		anear! for *anear.*
	B:	As in M
	H:	*its* written over *the*
	1850:	*sweet* for *Sweet*
	1853:	As in 1850
10	M:	*Country, Heaven,* for *country, heaven,*
	B:	*Heaven,* for *heaven,*
11	M:	*To where thou art or shall be, there or here—*
	B:	*To* changed to *For* (R)
		here: for *here;*
12	M:	*&* for *and*
		yesterday, . . for *yesterday,*
	B:	As in M
13	M:	*(The singing angels know!) are only dear*
	B:	*know!.) . .* for *know)*

VIII

1 What can I give thee back, O liberal
2 And princely giver, who has brought the gold
3 And purple of thine heart, unstained, untold,
4 And laid them on the outside of the wall
5 For such as I to take or leave withal,
6 In unexpected largesse? am I cold,
7 Ungrateful, that for these most manifold
8 High gifts, I render nothing back at all?
9 Not so; not cold,—but very poor instead.
10 Ask God who knows. For frequent tears have run
11 The colours from my life, and left so dead
12 And pale a stuff, it were not fitly done
13 To give the same as pillow to thy head.
14 Go farther! let it serve to trample on.

2-3 Untold means uncounted, not unspoken. Here is another example of E.B.B.'s frequent practice of taking an idea, phrase, or image of Browning's and using it for her own purposes, often reversing it in the process. On December 21, 1845, Browning began a paragraph with "Let me count my gold now—and rub off any speck that stays the full shining." (Kintner, I, 335.) Browning means his wealth in her, and the rubbing off of dust refers to an explanation he was about to make. E.B.B. took the notion of counting gold and ascribed to him the liberal, princely virtues of *not* counting his gold, that is, giving his wealth without calculation, not measuring out the fine qualities and the gift of his own self. Again, she reversed the "speck" into "unstained"—spotless.

4 outside the wall—her prison wall, presumably, as at the end she tells

him to go. In Sonnet III she is outside, in the darkness and leaning on a tree; in IV she is behind a broken casement in a ruin.

Heading

M: *Sonnets. VIII*

B: *Sonnet VIII*

    10 in upper right

H: *Sonnets from the Portuguese*

    VIII

The compositor's name, *Flose,* written at upper left

1   M: back for *back*,

2   M: And princely Giver, . . who hast brought the gold

      B: And princely Giver, . . who has brought the gold

      H: And princely giver, . . who hast brought the gold

      1850:   As in H

      1853:   giver, . . for *giver,*

3   B: unstained . . untold . . for *unstained, untold,*

4   M: wall, for *wall*

      H: As in M

      1850:   As in M

5   1850:   take, for *take*

6   M: unentreated for *unexpected*

          Largesse?. for *largesse?*

          cold,– for *cold,*

A Variorum Edition   29

6   B: As first two in M

      H: *Am* for *am*

      1850:   As in H

      1853:   As in H

7   M: *Ungrateful* . . for *ungrateful,*

      B: *Ungrateful,* . . for *ungrateful,*

9   M: *Not so—not cold—but very poor instead!*

      B: As in M

      H: *Not so. Not cold! but very poor instead!*

      1850:   *Not so. Not cold!—but very poor instead!*

      1853:   As in 1850

10   M: *knows!—* for *knows.*

      B: As in M

      H: *knows!.* for *knows.*

          for instead of *For*

      1850:   *knows!* for *knows.*

          for instead of *For*

      1853:   As in 1850

11   M: *life* written over *love*

          & for *and*

13   M: *To give the same as pillow to thine head!*

14   M: *Let it not serve* seems to have been changed to *It deserves* and both cancelled for *Let it serve*

      B: *Let* for *let*

      H: As in B

      1850:   As in B

14   1853:   As in B

IX

1 Can it be right to give what I can give?
2 To let thee sit beneath the fall of tears
3 As salt as mine, and hear the sighing years
4 Re-sighing on my lips renunciative
5 Through those infrequent smiles which fail to live
6 For all thy adjurations? O my fears,
7 That this can scarce be right! We are not peers,
8 So to be lovers; and I own, and grieve,
9 That givers of such gifts as mine are, must
10 Be counted with the ungenerous. Out, alas!
11 I will not soil thy purple with my dust,
12 Nor breathe my poison on thy Venice-glass,
13 Nor give thee any love . . . which were unjust.
14 Beloved, I only love thee! let it pass.

12 According to Porter and Clarke, "poison poured in Venetian glass was popularly supposed to shatter it, the quality of such glass being so fine as to feel at once the subtle element of death in the liquid." (III, 395.)

Heading

M: *Sonnets IX*

B: *Sonnet IX*

B: *11* in upper right

H: *Sonnets from the Portuguese*

IX

4	M:	*renunciative,* for *renunciative*
	B:	As in M
5	M:	*live,* for *live*
	1850:	*smiles,* for *smiles*
7	B:	*peers* for *peers,*
8	M:	Apparently, *To be as lo* cancelled and overwritten to read *So to be*

and written over first *And*

So to be lovers!—and I own & grieve

	B:	*and I own & grieve* for *and I own, and grieve,*
	H:	*So to be lovers; and I own and grieve*
	1850:	As in H
	1853:	As in H
10	M:	Apostrophe between *the* and *ungenerous*
11	M:	*dust,—* for *dust,*
12	M:	*Nor breathe my soul against thy Venice-glass, . .*
	B:	*Nor breathe my soul against thy Venice-glass,*
13	M:	*Nor give thee any love!. which were unjust!*
	B:	*Nor give thee any love: . . . which were unjust!*
14	M:	LOVE THEE! for *love thee!*
	B:	As in M

X

1 Yet, love, mere love, is beautiful indeed
2 And worthy of acceptation. Fire is bright,
3 Let temple burn, or flax. An equal light
4 Leaps in the flame from cedar-plank or weed.
5 And love is fire; and when I say at need
6 *I love thee* . . mark! . . *I love thee!* . . in thy sight
7 I stand transfigured, glorified aright,
8 With conscience of the new rays that proceed
9 Out of my face toward thine. There's nothing low
10 In love, when love the lowest: meanest creatures
11 Who love God, God accepts while loving so.
12 And what *I feel,* across the inferior features
13 Of what I *am,* doth flash itself, and show
14 How that great work of Love enhances Nature's.

---

8   Conscience here is used in the sense of consciousness, one of the meanings Dr. Johnson ascribes to it.

10-11   That is, when the meanest creatures love and recognize God, their love is worthy of "acceptation" since it has transformed them into something better.

Headings

M: *Sonnets. X*

34   Sonnets from the Portuguese

B: *Sonnet X*

12 in upper right

H: *Sonnets from the Portuguese*

Love's Temple cancelled (R)

X

1   M: *Yet love, mere love, is beautiful indeed,*

     B: *Yet love,* for *Yet, love,*

     H: *Love, merely love* changed to *Yet, love mere love,*

2   B: *bright* for *bright,*

3   M: *flax! an* for *flax. An*

     B: As in M

     H: *flax!* for *flax.*

     1850:   As in H

     1853:   As in H

4   M: *Leaps in the flame from cedar-raft or weed!*

     B: *Leaps in the flame from cedar-raft or weed.*

     H: *-raft* cancelled and *-plank* written above

5   M: *And Love is fire!—And when I say at need*

     B: *fire!—And* for *fire; and*

     H: *fire:* for *fire;*

     1850:   As in H

     1853:   As in H

6   M: <u>*'I Love Thee!'*</u> . . *mark!*. . 'I LOVE THEE'!. . *in thy sight*

7   M: *aright* for *aright,*

7	B:	As in M
9	M:	*Out my face to thine.* written over *From out thy face to mine.*
	B:	*to* for *toward*
10	M:	*lowest. Meanest creatures,* for *lowest: meanest creatures*
	B:	*lowest. Meanest* for *lowest: meanest*
11	M:	*Who love God, God accepts, for loving so.*
12	M:	Apostrophe between *the* and *inferior*
13	M:	*&* for *and*
14	B:	Comma after *Love* cancelled

XI

1　And therefore if to love can be desert,
2　I am not all unworthy. Cheeks as pale
3　As those you see, and trembling knees that fail
4　To bear the burden of a heavy heart,—
5　This weary minstrel-life that once was girt
6　To climb Aornus, and can scarce avail
7　To pipe now 'gainst the valley nightingale
8　A melancholy music,—why advert
9　To these things? O Beloved, it is plain
10　I am not of thy worth nor for thy place!
11　And yet, because I love thee, I obtain
12　From that same love this vindicating grace,
13　To live on still in love, and yet in vain, . .
14　To bless thee, yet renounce thee to thy face.

6　Aornus, according to Porter and Clarke, alludes to the Aornus of India, "a lonely, lofty rock whither only the birds of strong pinion soared to." (III, 395.)

Heading

M:　*Sonnets. XI*

B:　*Sonnet XI*

Sonnets from the Portuguese

B: *13* in upper right

H: *Sonnets from the Portuguese*

   XI

1   B: *desert* for *desert,*

3   M: *see,* . . for *see,*

4   B: *To bear a burden of a heavy heart,* . .

   H: *the* written over *a* before *burden*

   heart, for *heart,—*

   1850:   As in H

5   M: *This soul of a tired minstrel (better-girt*

6   M: *To climb Aornus') that can scarce avail*

   that written over *who*

7   M: *To pipe against the woodland nightingale,*

   B: *woodland* for *valley*

   H: As in B with *woodland* over erasures

   1850:   As in B

   1853:   As in B

8   M: *music.* . . . for *music,—*

   B: *music!* . . . . for *music,—*

   H: *music!* . . . for *music,—*

   1850:   *music!* . . for *music,—*

   1853:   As in 1850

9   B: *beloved,* for *Beloved,*

   H: As in B

10   M: *worth,* for *worth*

     H: *place:* for *place!*

     1850:   As in H

     1853:   As in H

11   M: *yet* for *yet,*

     B: *And yet because I love thee I obtain*

     H: *And yet because I love thee, I obtain*

     1850:   As in H

     1853:   As in B

12   M: *love,* for *love*

     B: *grace . .* for *grace,*

13   M: *To love on still in truth and yet in vain,—*

     B: *To live on still in love and yet in vain,* with *love* written over *truth*

     H: *love* for *love,*

14   M: *three,* for second *three*

     B: *To bless thee yet renounce thee, to thy face.*

     H: *To bless thee yet renounce thee to thy face.*

     1850:   As in H

     1853:   As in H

XII

1 Indeed this very love which is my boast,
2 And which, when rising up from breast to brow,
3 Doth crown me with a ruby large enow
4 To draw men's eyes and prove the inner cost, . .
5 This love even, all my worth, to the uttermost,
6 I should not love withal, unless that thou
7 Hadst set me an example, shown me how,
8 When first thine earnest eyes with mine were crossed,
9 And love called love. And thus, I cannot speak
10 Of love even, as a good thing of my own.
11 Thy soul hath snatched up mine all faint and weak,
12 And placed it by thee on a golden throne,—
13 And that I love (O soul, we must be meek!)
14 Is by thee only, whom I love alone.

3   *enow*—obsolete form of enough.

The genesis of the image in line 3 is again in a letter of Browning's. In replying to the letter in which E.B.B. discussed her feelings for her brother and father, Browning wrote:

> [. . .] from the beginning and at this moment I never dreamed of winning your *love* . . [. . .] nor, next to that, tho' long after, *would* I, if I *could,* supplant one of any of the affections that I know to have taken root in you—*that* great & solemn one, for instance . . I feel that if I could get myself *remade,* as if turned to gold, I WOULD not even then desire to become more than the mere setting to *that* diamond you must always wear: [. . .]
> (I, 191-92)

Sonnets from the Portuguese

Heading

M: *Sonnets XII*

B: *Sonnet XII*

    14 in upper right

H: *Sonnets from the Portuguese*

    G G

    449—vol. 2

    XII

1   M: *I think* for *Indeed*

    B: *Indeed this very Love,* written above cancelled line which read *And therefore this first Love,*

4   M: *To draw men's eyes, and prove the inner cost,—*

    B: *eyes,* for *eyes*

    H: As in B

    1850:   As in B

5   M: *This love even . . all my worth . . to the 'uttermost . .*

    B: *This love even . . all my worth . . to the uttermost, . .*

6   M: *withal—* for *withal,*

    B: *withal, . .* for *withal,*

7   M: *Had set me an exemplar, . . shown me how,*

    B: As in M

9   M: Each *love* with upper case l

10 M: *Of love even, as a good thing of my own!*

10	M:	Originally *Of love as something worthy of my own!* with *even,* written above *as* (R)
		something worthy cancelled (R) *as a good thing* written above
	B:	As in M
11	M:	& for *and*
		weak for *weak,*
	B:	& for *and*
12	B:	*throne:* for *throne,—*
13	M:	And that I love. (. . O Soul, I must be meek!)
	B:	And that I love . . (O soul, I must be meek!)
	H:	*love,* for *love*
		I for *we*
	1850:	As in H
	1853:	*I* for *we*
14	M:	*only* for *only,*

XIII

1 And wilt thou have me fashion into speech
2 The love I bear thee, finding words enough,
3 And hold the torch out, while the winds are rough,
4 Between our faces, to cast light on each?—
5 I drop it at thy feet. I cannot teach
6 My hand to hold my spirit so far off
7 From myself .. me .. that I should bring thee proof
8 In words, of love hid in me out of reach.
9 Nay, let the silence of my womanhood
10 Commend my woman-love to thy belief,—
11 Seeing that I stand unwon, however wooed,
12 And rend the garment of my life, in brief,
13 By a most dauntless, voiceless fortitude,
14 Lest one touch of this heart convey its grief.

Heading

M: *Sonnets XIII*

    Love's expression

B: *Sonnet XIII*

    15 in upper right

H: *Sonnets from the Portuguese*

H:	XIII	
2	M:	*The love I bear thee . . finding words enough?,*
		finding is written over an illegible word
3	M:	*And hold this torch out where the winds are rough*
	B:	*And hold the torch out where the winds are rough,*
		the written over *this*
	H:	*the* written over *this*
4	M:	*Between our faces to cast light on each?*
	B:	*each? . . for each?—*
5	M:	*-I drop* for *I drop*
8	M:	*In words, . . of love hid in me out of reach.*
	B:	*In words, . . of the love hid in me out of reach.*
9	M:	*Nay!* for *Nay,*
	B:	*Nay,—* for *Nay,*
10	M:	*Commend my woman's love to thy belief—*
11	M:	*And that I stand unwon though not unwooed—*
	B:	*unwon, however wooed,* written above cancelled *though not un* (R)
12	M:	*And rend the garment of my Life in brief*
	B:	*Rending the garment of my life, in brief,*
13	M:	*In* for *By*
	B:	As in M
	H:	*By* written over *In*
14	M:	*Lest one touch of its love should give thee its grief.*
	B:	*Lest one touch of this heart convey its grief.*

14 B: *this heart* written above cancelled *its love,*
   H: *heart,* for *heart*
   1850: As in H

XIV

1 If thou must love me, let it be for nought
2 Except for love's sake only. Do not say
3 'I love her for her smile . . her look . . her way
4 Of speaking gently, . . for a trick of thought
5 That falls in well with mine, and certes brought
6 A sense of pleasant ease on such a day'—
7 For these things in themselves, Belovèd, may
8 Be changed, or change for thee,—and love, so wrought,
9 May be unwrought so. Neither love me for
10 Thine own dear pity's wiping my cheeks dry,—
11 A creature might forget to weep, who bore
12 Thy comfort long, and lose thy love thereby!
13 But love me for love's sake, that evermore
14 Thou may'st love on, through love's eternity.

This theme goes through the letters from October 1845 to less than a month before the marriage. She feared particularly being loved out of compassion on the one hand, or for her poetry, apart from herself, on the other. The one is too concrete and likely, the other too abstract and what Elizabeth calls *a priori*. On October 24, 1845, E.B.B. wrote:

> [. . .] I have sometimes felt jealous of myself . . of my own infirmities, . . and thought that you cared for me only because your chivalry touched them with a silver sound—& that, without them, you would pass by on the other side:—why twenty times I have thought *that* & been vexed—ungrateful vexation!—

(I, 247)

50   *Sonnets from the Portuguese*

On November 12, 1845, she wrote

> Shall I tell you besides?—The first moment in which I seemed to admit to myself in a flash of lightening the *possibility* of your affection for me being more than dream-work . . the first moment was *that* when you intimated (as you have done since repeatedly) that you cared for me not for a reason, but because you cared for me.
>
> (I, 265)

Kinter points to letter 136 in which Browning had written "I love you because I *love* you; I see you 'once a week' because I cannot see you all day long;" and letter 148 in which he praises her "glorious genius," and suggests that these letters provoked not only the demurrer above but Sonnet XIV as well.

Heading

M: *Sonnets XIV*

      Love's causes

B: *Sonnet XIV*

      16 in upper right

H: *Sonnets from the Portuguese*

      XIV

1   M: *me* for *me,*

3   M: Double quotation marks

    B: As in M

    1850:   As in M

4   M: *gently—;* for *gently, . .*

    B: *gently . .;* for *gently, . .*

5   M: *Which falls in well with mine and certes brought*

A Variorum Edition 51

6   M: Double quotation marks

      B: As in M

      1850:   As in M

7   M: *things,* for *things*

      B: *beloved,* for *Belovèd,*

      H: Upper case *b* written over small letter

            No accent

      1850:   No accent

      1853:   As in 1850

8   M: *Be changed, or change for thee;... and love so wrought,*

      B: *Be changed, or change for thee,... and love so wrought*

      H: *love* for *love,*

      1850:   As in H

      1853:   As in H

9   M: *so!—* for *so.*

10 M: *Thine own dear pity' in wiping my cheeks dry!*

      B: As in M except *in* obliterated

      H: *dry,* for *dry,—*

      1850:   As in H

11 M: *I might forget to weep so, if I bore*

      B: *For one might well forget to weep, who bore*

            I might forget to weep, if, so, I bore cancelled

      H: *Since one might well forget to weep who bore*

      1850:   As in H

      1853:   As in H

12 M: *Such* for *Thy*

   B: *Thy comfort long, & lose thy love thereby.*

   H: *thereby,* for *thereby!*

   1850:   As in H

   1853:   As in H

14 M: *on* for *on,*

   B: As in M

   H: As in M

   1850:   As in M

   1853:   As in M

XV

1 Accuse me not, beseech thee, that I wear
2 Too calm and sad a face in front of thine;
3 For we two look two ways, and cannot shine
4 With the same sunlight on our brow and hair.
5 On me thou lookest, with no doubting care,
6 As on a bee shut in a crystalline,—
7 Since sorrow hath shut me safe in love's divine,
8 And to spread wing and fly in the outer air
9 Were most impossible failure, if I strove
10 To fail so. But I look on thee . . on thee . .
11 Beholding, besides love, the end of love,
12 Hearing oblivion beyond memory!
13 As one who sits and gazes from above,
14 Over the rivers to the bitter sea.

3   On September 19, 1845, E.B.B. wrote "[. . .] while you see from above & I from below, we cannot see the same thing in the same light" (I, 207).

6   *crystalline,* according to Porter and Clarke, is not akin to amber but means a glass vessel. It is not Browning who has shut her in the vessel but her poor health and family circumstances, the "sorrow" of the sonnet.

11 This fear persisted for many months. "I am frightened . . I tremble! When you come to know me as well as I know myself, what can save me, do you think from disappointing & displeasing you? I ask the question, & find no answer—" (I, 324), Elizabeth wrote on December 18, 1845.

54 *Sonnets from the Portuguese*

Heading

M: *Sonnet. XV*

B: *Sonnet XV*

   17 in upper right

H: *Sonnets from the Portuguese*

   Two titles, one written over the other and both cancelled.

   XV

   The compositor's name, *Footman*, at upper left

1 M: *thee!,* for *thee,*

2 M: *Too calm & sad a face in front of thine!*

   B: *Too calm & sad a face in front of thine,*

3 M: *&* for *and*

   B: *ways* for *ways,*

4 M: *With the same sunlight on our brow & hair!*

   B: *&* for *and*

5 M: *Thou lookest, sweet, on me, without a care, . .*

   B: *Thou lookest, sweet, on me, without a care*

   H: *doubting* cancelled and restored above line

6 M: *crystalline, . .* for *crystalline,—*

   B: As in M

7 M: *For sorrow shuts me safe in love's divine,—*

   B: *For* instead of *Since*

   H: As in B

7   1850:   As in B

    1853:   As in B

8   M: & for second *and*

    B: As in M

9   1853:   *failure* for *failure,*

10   M: But *I* look on *thee* . . on *thee* . .

11   M: Beholding besides love, the end of love . .

    B: Beholding besides love, the end of love,

12   M: *memory* . . for *memory!*

    B: *memory* . . . for *memory!*

    H: As in B

    1850:   As in B

    1853:   As in B

13   M: *above* for *above,*

    B: As one who sits & gazes, from above,

    H: *gazes,* for *gazes*

    1850:   As in H

XVI

1 And yet, because thou overcomest so,
2 Because thou art more noble and like a king,
3 Thou canst prevail against my fears and fling
4 Thy purple round me, till my heart shall grow
5 Too close against thine heart, henceforth to know
6 How it shook when alone. Why, conquering
7 May prove as lordly and complete a thing
8 In lifting upward, as in crushing low!
9 And as a vanquished soldier yields his sword
10 To one who lifts him from the bloody earth,—
11 Even so, Belovèd, I at last record,
12 Here ends my strife. If *thou* invite me forth,
13 I rise above abasement at the word.
14 Make thy love larger to enlarge my worth.

3-4 This image probably also originated with Browning who wrote on January 6, 1846, "[. . .] you take me in your mantle, and we shine together [. . .]" (I, 365).

8 This recurring idea of the poet being lifted to worthiness by a "kingly" and "princely" lover is another ironic reversal of a phrase of Browning's. On November 9, 1845, he wrote that he did not want her to neglect her poetry for his sake, but if she could be both poet and lover, it would be well: "Yet, if you can lift me with one hand, while the other suffices to crown you—there is queenliness in *that* too!" (I, 262).

58   *Sonnets from the Portuguese*

                              ⌒
                              ∫

Heading

M: *Sonnet XVI*

B: *Sonnet XVI.*

      18 in upper right

H: *Sonnets from the Portuguese*

      XVI

1   M: *And yet because thou art above me so,*

      B: *And yet . . because thou overcomest so, . .*

2   M: *Because thou art more strong, & like a king,*

      B: *Because thou art more princely & like a king,*

3   M: *&* for *and*

      B: As in M

4   M: *me* for *me,*

5   M: *Too close against thy heart to henceforth know*

      B: *to henceforth know*

      H: *to* cancelled before *henceforth*

6   M: *Its separate trembling pulse. Oh, conquering*

7   M: *May prove as noble & complete a thing*

      B: As in M

8   M: *In lifting upward as in beating low!*

      B: *upward* for *upward,*

      H: *In lifting upward as in crushing low:*

      1850:   As in H

A Variorum Edition 59

8   1853:   As in H

9   M: *And as a soldier, struck down by a sword,*

      B: As in M

      H: *And, as a soldier struck down by a sword*

      1850:   As in H

      1853:   As in H

10 M: *Cries 'Here my strife ends,' & sinks dead to earth,—*

            battle cancelled for *strife* written above, and *dead* inserted

      B: *May cry 'My strife ends here', and sink to earth,* ...

      H: *May cry 'My strife ends here,' and sink to earth,*

      1850:   *May cry, "My strife ends here," and sink to earth,*

      1853:   As in 1850 with single quotation marks

11 M: *Even so, beloved, I, at last, record* ..

            yield thee my cancelled and *at last* written above

      B: *beloved* for *Belovèd*

      H: *Beloved* for *Belovèd*

      1850:   As in H

      1853:   As in H

12 M: *'My doubts end here—'* written above cancelled *'Here ends my fear!'*

      B: ... *Here ends my doubt!*

      H: *Here ends my doubt!*

      1850:   As in H

      1853:   As in H

13 M: *word!* for *word.*

      B: *abasement,* for *absement*

14   B: *my* written over *thy* before *worth*

XVII

1 My poet, thou canst touch on all the notes
2 God set between His After and Before,
3 And strike up and strike off the general roar
4 Of the rushing worlds, a melody that floats
5 In a serene air purely. Antidotes
6 Of medicated music, answering for
7 Mankind's forlornest uses, thou canst pour
8 From thence into their ears. God's will devotes
9 Thine to such ends, and mine to wait on thine.
10 How, Dearest, wilt thou have me for most use?
11 A hope, to sing by gladly? . . or a fine
12 Sad memory, with thy songs to interfuse?
13 A shade, in which to sing . . . of palm or pine?
14 A grave, on which to rest from singing? . . Choose.

2 *His After and Before*—life on earth, i.e. after birth and before death.

13 *palm* or *pine*—pine presumably stands for death. Thre is no doubt that palm stands for life, well-being, joy. On Palm Sunday, for example, the palm symbolizes victory over death. E.B.B. frequently uses the word in her letters to symbolize the life the Browning's would have together in Italy.

Sonnet XVII is missing from the Morgan manuscript sequence.

Heading

B: *Sonnet XVIII*

    20 at upper right

H: *Sonnets from the Portuguese*

    XVII

3   B: & for second *and*

6   B: *music* for *music,*

9   H: *thine!* for *thine.*

    1850:   As in H

    1853:   As in H

10 B: *dearest,* for *Dearest,*

12 B: *interfuse?* . . for *interfuse?*

    H: As in B

    1850:   As in B

    1853:   As in B

XVIII

1 I never gave a lock of hair away
2 To a man, Dearest, except this to thee,
3 Which now upon my fingers thoughtfully
4 I ring out to the full brown length and say
5 'Take it.' My day of youth went yesterday;
6 My hair no longer bounds to my foot's glee,
7 Nor plant I it from rose or myrtle-tree,
8 As girls do, any more. It only may
9 Now shade on two pale cheeks, the mark of tears,
10 Taught drooping from the head that hangs aside
11 Through sorrow's trick. I thought the funeral-shears
12 Would take this first, but Love is justified,—
13 Take it thou, .. finding pure, from all those years,
14 The kiss my mother left here when she died.

---

1   On November 24, 1845, E.B.B. wrote Browning that "I never gave away what you ask me to give *you*, to a human being, except my nearest relatives & once or twice to female friends, .." (Kintner, I, 289.)

7   Porter and Clarke write "nor does she plant in her hair now sprigs from the rose or the myrtle tree." (III, 397.)

11 Porter and Clarke explain this as "an allusion to the Greek and Roman custom of cutting the hair, at death." (III, 397.)

I am indebted to Professor William S. Peterson for the information that this lock of hair is now in the Keats-Shelley House in Rome. See *TLS*, 23 April, 1970, pp. 457-58.

Heading

M: *Sonnet XIX*

B: *Sonnet XIX*

  21 at upper right

H: *Sonnets from the Portuguese*

  XVIII

2 M: *dearest,* for *Dearest,*

  B: As in M

4 M: *&* for *and*

5 M: *yesterday—* for *yesterday;*

  B: As in M

  1850: Double quotation marks

6 M: *glee, . .* for *glee,*

7 M: *it,* for *it*

  B: *myrtle tree* for *myrtle-tree,*

9 M: *Now, shade, on two pale cheeks, the mark of tears,*

  B: *tears* for *tears,*

11 M: *funeral shears* for *funeral-shears*

  B: As in M

12 M: *Would take this first! but Love is justified!*

  B: *Would take this first,—but Love is justified.*

  H: *Would take this first; but Love is justified:*

  1850: As in H

12 1853: *Would take this first, but Love is justified;*
13 M: *Take it, thou—finding pure from all those years,*
    B: *Take it, thou, . . finding pure from all those years*

XIX

1 The soul's Rialto hath its merchandise;
2 I barter curl for curl upon that mart,
3 And from my poet's forehead to my heart,
4 Receive this lock which outweighs argosies,—
5 As purply black, as erst, to Pindar's eyes,
6 The dim purpureal tresses gloomed athwart
7 The nine white Muse-brows. For this counterpart, . .
8 Thy bay-crown's shade, Belovèd, I surmise,
9 Still lingers on thy curl, it is so black!
10 Thus, with a fillet of smooth-kissing breath,
11 I tie the shadow safe from gliding back,
12 And lay the gift where nothing hindereth,
13 Here on my heart, as on thy brow, to lack
14 No natural heat till mine grows cold in death.

1   *Rialto*—an Exchange or mart, from the quarter of Venice in which the Exchange was situated. Porter and Clarke feel the imagery is an echo of Shakespeare's in *The Merchant of Venice;* the argosies outweighed by this curl are Antonio's.

5-6 *purply-black . . . purpureal tresses*—in his translation of 1822 Abraham Moore translates the relevant lines from Pindar, the Greek lyric poet (b. Thebes c. 518, d. c. 483 BC), in the following manner

> Golden Lyre, Appollo's care
> Thy aid with violet tresses crown'd
>   "Pythian I"

68   *Sonnets from the Portuguese*

The discussion of this exchange in the correspondence indicates that these two sonnets were written at the end of November 1845.

Heading

M: *Sonnet XX*

B: *Sonnet XX*

    22 at upper right

H: *Sonnets from the Portuguese*

    XIX

1   *merchandise:* for *merchandise;*

2   M: *mart;* for *mart,*

    B: As in M

    H: As in M

    1850:   As in M

    1853:   As in M

3   B: *heart* for *heart,*

4   B: *argosies— . .* for *argosies,—*

5   M: *And* for *As*

    B: *As purply black as erst to Pindar's eyes*

    H: *As purply black, as erst to Pindar's eyes*

    1850:   As in H

    1853:   As in H

6   M: First written *The dim curls floated mystical athwart* with *curls* cancelled and *purpureal tresses* inserted above the line

A Variorum Edition 69

6   M: *floated* and *mystical* cancelled and *floated that bound drawn gloomed* written above the line and only *gloomed* retained.

7   M: *For* written over another word

     B: *counterpart, . . .* for *counterpart, . .*

     H: As in B

8   M: *my poet* for *Belovèd*

     B: *Thy bay-crown's shade, beloved, I surmise*

     H: *Beloved* for *Belovèd*

     1850:   As in H

     1853:   As in H

10   M: *Thus with the fillet of a smooth-kissed breath*

         with the written over illegible words

         First written *And with the* cancelled

     B: As in M

11   M: *the* written over *its*

12   M: *Then lay the curl where nothing hindereth*

         The first and cancelled version reads *Let it lie hencefort, where Love counselleth,*

     B: *And lay the curl where nothing hindereth*

     H: *gift* written over erasure

13   M: *Here on my heart as on thy brow, to lacks*

         Cancelled *Laid* above *Here* which is written over *Over*

         to written over *it*

     B: *heart* for *heart,*

     1850:   As in B

     1853:   As in B

14 M: *No natural heart till I grow cold in death.*
    B: As in M

XX

1 Beloved, my Beloved, when I think
2 That thou wast in the world a year ago,
3 What time I sate alone here in the snow
4 And saw no footprint, heard the silence sink
5 No moment at thy voice, . . but, link by link,
6 Went counting all my chains, as if that so
7 They never could fall off at any blow
8 Struck by thy possible hand. . . . why, thus I drink
9 Of life's great cup of wonder! Wonderful,
10 Never to feel thee thrill the day or night
11 With personal act or speech,—nor ever cull
12 Some prescience of thee with the blossoms white
13 Thou sawest growing! Atheists are as dull,
14 Who cannot guess God's presence out of sight.

Elizabeth used the image of the footprint several times in the correspondence, but it is most closely allied to this sonnet in the following letter of January 10, 1846:

> [. . .] Shall I tell you?—it seems to me, to myself, that no man was ever before to any woman what you are to me—the fulness must be in proportion, you know, to the vacancy . . & only *I* know what was behind . . the long wilderness *without* the footstep, . . without the blossoming rose . . and the capacity for happiness, like a black gaping hole, before the silver flooding.
> (I, 376)

The idea of so nearly missing this experience is associated with Elizabeth's circumscribed existence generally, and appears again in Sonnet XXVI.

Heading

M: *Sonnet XXI*

B: *Sonnet XXI*

    23 at upper right

H: *Sonnets from the Portuguese*

    XX

1   M: lower case *b* in second *Beloved*

       B: As in M

       H: As in M

2   M: *wert* for *wast*

       B: *a year* written over *in other*

            ago for *ago,*

5   B: *No moment at thy voice, . . . but link by link*

       H: *but link by link*

       1850:   As in H

       1853:   As in H

6   B: *chains* for *chains,*

       H: As in B

       1850:   As in B

       1853:   As in B

8   M: *Struck by thy possible hand . . . why thus I drink*

       B: As in M

9   M: *Wonderful, . .* for *Wonderful,*

A Variorum Edition 73

9   B: *Wonderful* for *Wonderful,*

      H: *wonder.* for *wonder!*

      1850:   As in H

      1853:   As in H

13 M: *We both saw* written above line

          Thou too saw growing has *too* cancelled and *saw* changed to *sawest*

          Cancelled word between *are* and *as*

      B: *Thou sawest growing. Atheists are as dull*

XXI

1 Say over again, and yet once over again,
2 That thou dost love me. Though the word repeated
3 Should seem 'a cuckoo-song,' as thou dost treat it,
4 Remember never to the hill or plain,
5 Valley and wood, without her cuckoo-strain,
6 Comes the fresh Spring in all her green completed.
7 Beloved, I, amid the darkness greeted
8 By a doubtful spirit-voice, in that doubt's pain
9 Cry . . 'Speak once more . . thou lovest!' Who can fear
10 Too many stars, though each in heaven shall roll—
11 Too many flowers, though each shall crown the year?
12 Say thou dost love me, love me, love me—toll
13 The silver iterance!—only minding, Dear,
14 To love me also in silence, with thy soul.

3   This sonnet was probably written in December 1845. Having written a devastating critique of James Russell Lowell's *Conversations on Some of the Old Poets,* Browning continued, on December 19, 1845:

> No, I will say the true thing against myself—and it is, that—when I turn from what is in my mind, and determine to write about anybody's book to avoid writing what I love & love & love again my own, dearest love—because of the cuckoo-song of it,—*then,* I shall be in no better humour with that book than with Mr. Lowell's! (I, 329.)

76   *Sonnets from the Portuguese*

Heading

M: *Sonnet XXII*

    Love's repetitions.

B: *Sonnet XXII*

    25 at upper right

H: *Sonnets from the Portuguese*

    Repetitions cancelled

    XXI

1   M: *Beloved, say again & yet again*

    B: As in M

    H: *Say over again and yet once over again*

    1850:   As in H

    1853:   As in H

2   M: *me!* for *me.*

3   M: *Should seem a cuckoo-song as thou dost mete it,*

    B: As in M

    1850:   Double quotation marks

4   M: *Remember, never to the hill & plain,*

    B: *Remember, never to the hill & plain*

5   M: *&* written over *or* after *Valley*

    B: *Valley & wood, without her cuckoo-strain*

6   M: *Comes the sweet spring in all her green completed!*

    B: *Comes the sweet spring in all her green, completed.*

A Variorum Edition 77

6   H: *completed!* for *completed.*

       1850:   As in H

       1853:   As in H

7   M: *Beloved! I amid the darkness greeted*

       B: *Beloved!*

8   M: *By a doubtful spirit-voice, in mortal pain,*

       B: *in the doubt's pain* with *the doubt's* written above cancelled *mortal*

       H: *that* written over *the*

9   M: *Cry . . "Speak once more . . . thou lovest!.' Who can fear*

       B: *Cry . . speak once more . . thou lovest! Who can fear*

       H: As in B

       1850:   As in B

       1853:   As in B

10   M: *should roll?* for *shall roll—*

       B: *should roll . .* for *shall roll—*

11   M: *should crown* written above *adorn*

       B: *should crown* for *shall crown*

12   M: *me!—* for last *me—*

       B: *me . . .* for last *me—*

       H: *me . .* for last *me—*

13   M: *The silver iterance! only minding, dear,*

       B: *dear,* for *Dear,*

14   M: Apostrophe between *also* and *in*

XXII

1 When our two souls stand up erect and strong,
2 Face to face, silent, drawing nigh and nigher,
3 Until the lengthening wings break into fire
4 At either curvéd point,—what bitter wrong
5 Can the earth do to us, that we should not long
6 Be here contented? Think. In mounting higher,
7 The angels would press on us, and aspire
8 To drop some golden orb of perfect song
9 Into our deep, dear silence. Let us stay
10 Rather on earth, Belovèd,—where the unfit
11 Contrarious moods of men recoil away
12 And isolate pure spirits, and permit
13 A place to stand and love in for a day,
14 With darkness and the death-hour rounding it.

Heading

M: *Sonnet XXIII*

   Love's refuge.

B: *Sonnet XXIII*

   26 at upper right

H: *Sonnets from the Portuguese*

Sonnets from the Portuguese

H: XXII

1   M: & for *and*

    B: As in M

2   M: & for *and*

    B: As in M

3   M: *Until their widening wings break into fire* with *their* written over *the*

    B: *their* for *the*

    H: As in B

4   M: *point, . . . for point,—*

    B: *At either curvèd point, ... what bitter wrong,*

5   M: *Can earth* for *Can the earth*

6   M: *Think, . . in* for *Think. In*

    B: As in M

7   M: *The angels would press on us & aspire*

9   M: *deep* for *deep,*

10 M: *Rather on earth, beloved!—where the' unfit*

    B: *beloved! . .* for *Belovèd,—*

    H: *Beloved,—* for *Belovèd,—*

    1850: As in H

    1853: As in H

13 M: & for *and*

    B: *A place to stand & love in, for a day, . .*

14 M: *With darkness and the deathhour rounding it!*

    darkness cancels an illegible word

14 B: *death hour* for *death-hour*
    H: As in B

XXIII

1 Is it indeed so? If I lay here dead,
2 Would'st thou miss any life in losing mine?
3 And would the sun for thee more coldly shine,
4 Because of grave-damps falling round my head?
5 I marvelled, my Belovèd, when I read
6 Thy thought so in the letter. I am thine—
7 But .. *so* much to thee? Can I pour thy wine
8 While my hands tremble? Then my soul, instead
9 Of dreams of death, resumes life's lower range.
10 Then, love me, Love! look on me .. breathe on me!
11 As brighter ladies do not count it strange,
12 For love, to give up acres and degree,
13 I yield the grave for thy sake, and exchange
14 My near sweet view of Heaven, for earth with thee!

Heading

M: *Sonnet XXIV*

   Love's sacrifice

B: *Sonnet XXIV*

   27 at upper right

H: *Sonnets from the Portuguese*

Sonnets from the Portuguese

H: XXIII

2   M: *Wouldst thou* miss any life in losing mine?

    B: *life,* for *life*

    H: *mine,* for *mine?*

    1850:   As in H

    1853:   As in H

5   M: *belovèd,* for *Belovèd,*

    B: As in M

    H: As in M

    1850:   *Belovèd,* for *Belovèd,*

    1853:   As in 1850

6   M: *Thy thought so in the letter!—I am thine!*

7   M: *But so much to thee!—*

    B: *But . . . so much to thee? Can I pour thy wine,*

8   M: *While my hands tremble?—Then my soul instead*

9   M: *the* for *life's*

    B: *range!* for *range.*

    H: As in B

    1850:   As in B

    1853:   As in B

10 M: *Then, love me, love! look on me, breathe on me!*

    B: *Then, . . love me, love!*

11 M: *As* written over *Since* and both cancelled (R)

         As written in the margin

A Variorum Edition 85

11   M: *strange* for *strange,*

       B: *And brighter* cancelled and *As a brighter* with *a* cancelled written above

12   M: *For love to give up lands,—and high degree,*

            For love written in the margin

            for love cancelled after *lands*

            And degree cancelled

       B: *For love to give up lands and high degree,*

       H: *acres* written over erasure

13   M: *I* written next to heavy cancellation, possibly capital Y

14   M: *My near sweet view of Heaven for earth with thee.*

       B: *My near sweet view of Heaven . . for earth with <u>thee!</u>*

XXIV

1 Let the world's sharpness like a clasping knife
2 Shut in upon itself and do no harm
3 In this close hand of Love, now soft and warm,
4 And let us hear no sound of human strife
5 After the click of the shutting. Life to life—
6 I lean upon thee, Dear, without alarm,
7 And feel as safe as guarded by a charm
8 Against the stab of worldlings, who if rife
9 Are weak to injure. Very whitely still
10 The lilies of our lives may reassure
11 Their blossoms from their roots, accessible
12 Alone to heavenly dews that drop not fewer;
13 Growing straight, out of man's reach, on the hill.
14 God only, who made us rich, can make us poor.

Heading

M: *Sonnet XXV*

B: *Sonnet XXV*

    28 at upper right

H: *Sonnets from the Portuguese*

    XXIV

2	M:	& for *and*
	B:	*itself,* for *itself*
3	M:	*Love now soft & warm,—*
	B:	As in M
	H:	*warm;* for *warm,*
	1850:	As in H
4	M:	*mortal* for *human*
	B:	As in M
	H:	*strife,* for *strife*
	1850:	As in H
5	M:	*life,* for second *life—*
6	M:	Lower case *d* in *Dear*
	B:	As in M
7	M:	*And feel as safe, as witches by a charm,*
		First five words written over an erasure
		by written over *in*
	B:	*And feel as safe as witches by a charm,*
	H:	*And feel as safe as guarded by a charm,*
	1850:	As in H
	1853:	As in H
8	M:	*Against the stabs of worldlings, who are rife*
	B:	As in M
	H:	*Against the stab of worldlings who if rife*
		if written above cancelled *are*
	1850:	As in H

A Variorum Edition 89

8   1853:   As in H

9   M: *But weak to attain us. Very whitely, still*

            us written over *me*

            Good with all their ill! cancelled

            Very whitely, pure and still written above the line with *pure* cancelled

     B: *But weak to attain us. Very whitely, still,*

     H: *But* cancelled and *Are* written above

11   M: *Their blossoms from their roots: —their cups they fill*

     B: *Their blossoms, from their roots: . . their cups, they fill,*

     H: *Their blossoms from their roots! accessible*

            accessible written above cancelled *their cups they fill* (R)

     1850:   As in H

     1853:   As in H

12   M: *From Heaven's amreeta fatal to the impure,*

     B: As in M

     H: *Alone, to heavenly dews that drop not fewer;* written above cancelled line as in M

13   M: *And grow straight, out of man's reach, on the hill!*

     B: As in M

     H: *Growing* written above cancelled *And grow*

XXV

1 A heavy heart, Belovèd, have I borne
2 From year to year until I saw thy face,
3 And sorrow after sorrow took the place
4 Of all those natural joys as lightly worn
5 As the stringed pearls . . each lifted in its turn
6 By a beating heart at dance-time. Hopes apace
7 Were changed to long despairs, till God's own grace
8 Could scarcely lift above the world forlorn
9 My heavy heart. Then *thou* didst bid me bring
10 And let it drop adown thy calmly great
11 Deep being! Fast it sinketh, as a thing
12 Which its own nature doth precipitate,
13 While thine doth close above it, mediating
14 Betwixt the stars and the unaccomplished fate.

Heading

M: *Sonnet XXVI*

B: *Sonnet XXVI*

    29 at upper right

H: *Sonnets from the Portuguese*

    XXV

1	M:	*beloved,* for *Belovèd,*
	B:	As in M
	H:	*Beloved,* for *Belovèd,*
	1850:	As in H
	1853:	As in H
2	M:	*face,—* for *face,*
	B:	*face:* for *face,*
4	M:	*hopes,* for *joys*
	B:	*joys,* with *natural* inserted before and above
5	M:	*pearls,* for *pearls . .*
	B:	*turn,* for *turn*
6	M:	*By a beating heart at feast-time. Joys apace*
7	M:	*till* written over *all*
	B:	*despairs, . . .* for *despairs,*
	H:	*despairs, . .* for *despairs,*
	1850:	As in H
	1853:	As in H
8	B:	*forlorn,* for *forlorn*
9	M:	*heart!* for *heart.*
12	M:	*doth* written over *did* (R)
		precipitate, . . for *precipitate,*
	B:	As in M
14	M:	*&* for *and*

XXVI

1 I lived with visions for my company,

2 Instead of men and women, years ago,

3 And found them gentle mates, nor thought to know

4 A sweeter music than they played to me.

5 But soon their trailing purple was not free

6 Of this world's dust,—their lutes did silent grow,

7 And I myself grew faint and blind below

8 Their vanishing eyes. Then THOU didst come . . to be,

9 Belovèd, what they seemed. Their shining fronts,

10 Their songs, their splendours, (better, yet the same,

11 As river-water hallowed into fonts)

12 Met in thee, and from out thee overcame

13 My soul with satisfaction of all wants—

14 Because God's gifts put man's best dreams to shame.

Before they met, E.B.B. wrote Browning her views of her life:

> And what you say of society draws me on to many comparative thoughts of your life & mine. You seem to have drunken the cup of life full, with the sun shining on it. I have lived only inwardly,—or with *sorrow*, for a strong emotion. Before this seclusion of my illness, I was secluded still—& there are few of the youngest women in the world who have not seen more, heard more, known more, of society, than I, who am scarcely to be called young now. I grew up in the country . . had no social opportunities, . . had my heart in books & poetry, . . & my experience, in reveries. My sympathies drooped towards the ground like an untrained honeysuckle—& but for *one* . . in my own house . . but of this I cannot speak. It was a lonely

94   *Sonnets from the Portuguese*

life—growing green like the grass around it. Books and dreams were what I lived in—& domestic life only seemed to buzz gently around, like the bees about the grass. And so time passed, and passed—and afterwards, when my illness came & I seemed to stand at the edge of the world with all done, & no prospect (as appeared at one time) of ever passing the threshold of one room again,—why then, I turned to thinking with some bitterness (after the greatest sorrow of my life had given me room & time to breathe) that I had stood blind in this temple I was about to leave . . that I had seen no Human nature, that my brothers & sisters of the earth were *names* to me, . . that I had beheld no great mountain or river—nothing in fact. I was as a man dying who had not read Shakespeare . . & it was too late!—do you understand? And do you also know what a disadvantage this ignorance is to my art—Why, if I live on & yet do not escape from this seclusion, do you not perceive that I labour under signal disadvantages . . that I am, in a manner, as a *blind poet*? Certainly, there is a compensation to a degree. I have had much of the inner life—& from the habit of selfconsciousness of selfanalysis, I make great guesses at Human Nature in the main. But how willingly I would as a poet exchange some of this lumbering, ponderous, helpless knowledge of books, for some experience of life & man [. . .]

(I, 41)

1-8   This theme runs through the correspondence from February through August, 1845. It is notably present in letters 6, 14 (where it is most fully developed), 17, 37, 77, and 87 in Kintner's edition.

Heading

M: *Sonnet XXVII*

B: *Sonnet XXVII*

      30 at upper right

H: *Sonnets from the Portuguese*

      XXVI

      Visions and realities cancelled

1   M: *I lived with Dreams for all my company,*

      B: As in M but without the comma

A Variorum Edition

1 H: *company* for *company,*

   1850:   As in H

   1853:   As in H

2 M: & for *and*

   B: As in M

3 M: & for *nor*

   B: *nor* written above cancelled *and*

4 M: *None sweeter music than they played for me.*

   None written above cancelled *Not*

   B: *A* written above cancelled *None*

6 M: *Of this world's dust, . . their lutes did silent grow,*

   did written above cancelled *waxed*

   grow written over *now*

   B: *dust;* for *dust,—*

7 M: & for *and*

   B: As in M

8 M: *Their vanishing eyes! Then Thou didst come, to <u>be</u>,*

   B: *Then <u>thou</u> didst come . . to <u>be</u>,*

   H: <u>*be,*</u>

   1850:   As in H

   1853:   As in H

9 M: *Beloved, what they <u>seemed!</u> Their shining fronts*

   B: As in M with comma after *fronts*

   H: *Beloved, what they <u>seemed.</u>*

   1850:   As in H

9	1853:	As in 1850
10	M:	*Their songs, their splendours . . (better, yet the same . .*
	B:	*Their songs, their splendours, . . . (better, yet the same, . .*
	H:	*Their songs, their splendours . . (better, yet the same, . .*
	1850:	As in H
	1853:	As in H
11	M:	*As river-water consecrate in fonts . . .)*
		consecrate in written above cancelled *taken into*
	B:	*fonts . .)* for *fonts)*
	H:	As in B
	1850:	As in B
	1853:	As in B
12	M:	*Met in thee, & from out thee, overcame*
	B:	*Met in thee, and, from out thee, overcame*
13	M:	*all* written over *its*
14	M:	*may* and *shall* cancelled before *put*
		best inserted before *dreams*

XXVII

1 My own belovèd, who hast lifted me
2 From this drear flat of earth where I was thrown,
3 And, in betwixt the languid ringlets, blown
4 A life-breath, till the forehead hopefully
5 Shines out again, as all the angels see,
6 Before thy saving kiss! My own, my own,
7 Who camest to me when the world was gone,
8 And I who looked for only God, found *thee!*
9 I find thee; I am safe, and strong, and glad.
10 As one who stands in dewless asphodel,
11 Looks backward on the tedious time he had
12 In the upper life,—so I, with bosom-swell,
13 Make witness, here, between the good and bad,
14 That Love, as strong as Death, retrieves as well.

10   *asphodel*—a genus of liliaceous plants with beautiful flowers, native to the south of Europe. Made an immortal flower by the poets and said to cover the fields of Elysium. It is also to be found in Hades, according to Homer, who has Achilleus walking away through fields of asphodel after Odysseus reassures him about his son. (*Odyssey,* Book XI, 539.)

Heading

M: *Sonnet 28*

Sonnets from the Portuguese

B: *Sonnet XXVIII*

    31 at upper right

H: *Sonnets from the Portuguese*

    XXVII

1   M: *beloved!* for *belovèd,*

       B: *beloved,* for *belovèd,*

       H: As in B

       1850:   *Beloved,* for *belovèd,*

       1853:   As in B

2   M: *tears* for *earth*

       B: *thrown,—* for *thrown,*

           earth written above cancelled *tears*

3   M: *And in betwixt my heavy ringlets, blown*

       B: As in M but without the comma

       H: *And* for *And,*

       1850:   As in H

       1853:   As in H

4   M: *A lifebreath, as a southwind swells the sea,*

       B: *A lifebreath, till my forehead hopefully* last three words written above heavily cancelled words

5   M: *Letting the forehead shine more hopefully*

       B: *Shines out again as all the angels see,* written above cancelled M line

6   M: *Against thy saving kiss .. my own, my own ..*

       B: *Against thy saving kiss! .. My own, my own ..*

A Variorum Edition 99

8 M: *And I who looked for only God, find thee!—*

   B: *I,* for *I*

9 M: *I find thee—I am safe & strong & glad!*

   B: *I find thee! I am safe, & strong, & glad!*

   find written over *found, find* also pencilled in above

   H: *thee:* for *thee;*

   1850: As in H

   1853: As in H

10 M: *asphodel* for *asphodel,*

   B: As in M

   H: As in M

   1850: As in M

   1853: As in M

11 M: *to* for *on*

12 M: *In the upper life . . so I with bosom-swell*

   B: *life . .* for *life,—*

   H: As in B

   1850: As in B

   1853: As in B

13 M: *Make witness here between the good & bad,*

   Make witness here written above cancelled *Here* and another word

   B: As in M

   H: As in M

   1850: As in M

   1853: *here* for *here,*

14   M: *Love* for *Love*,

XXVIII

1 My letters! all dead paper, . . mute and white!—
2 And yet they seem alive and quivering
3 Against my tremulous hands which loose the string
4 And let them drop down on my knee to-night.
5 This said, . . he wished to have me in his sight
6 Once, as a friend: this fixed a day in spring
7 To come and touch my hand . . . a simple thing,
8 Yet I wept for it!—this, . . the paper's light . .
9 Said, *Dear, I love thee;* and I sank and quailed
10 As if God's future thundered on my past.
11 This said, *I am thine*—and so its ink has paled
12 With lying at my heart that beat too fast.
13 And this . . . O Love, thy words have ill availed,
14 If, what this said, I dared repeat at last!

5   "[. . .] do you know I was once not very far from seeing—really seeing you? [. . .] —and I feel as at some untoward passage in my travels—as if I had been close, so close, to some world's-wonder in chapel or crypt, [. . .]"
January 10, 1845 (I, 3-4.)

"[. . .] but I will joyfully wait for the delight of your friendship and the spring, and my Chapel-sight after all!"
January 13, 1845 (I, 7.)

6   "I will call at 2 on Tuesday—"
May 16, 1845 (I, 68.)

8   "When I wrote that letter to let you come the first time, do you

know, the tears ran down my cheeks .."
October 13, 1845 (I, 255.)

8-14   These feelings were expressed for the first time in a letter Browning wrote after the first visit. Elizabeth forbade any further discussion of that kind and Browning destroyed the letter, having asked for it back. Soon afterwards oblique references to the state of his feelings begin to reappear in the correspondence, culminating in the following declaration on August 30, 1845: "Let me say now—*this only once—* that I loved you from my soul, and gave you my life, so much of it as you would take,—and all that is *done,* and not altered now: [. . .]"
(I, 176.)

It was, of course, not *"this only once"*—such declarations came frequently in the subsequent months, as Sonnet XX testifies.

Heading

M: *Sonnet 29th*

B: *Sonnet XXIX*

    32 at upper right

H: *Sonnets from the Portuguese*

    XXVIII

    at upper left: *HH*

        465

        Vol. 2

1   M: *My letters! all dead paper, mute & white!*

     B: *My letters! all dead paper, . . mute & white!*

     H: As in B

2   M: *And* written over *Yet* at the beginning of the line

        & for second *and*

3   M: *Against my trembling hands, which loose the string*

    H: *hands,* for *hands*

    1850:   As in H

4   M: *tonight.* for *to-night.*

    B: As in M

    H: As in M

5   M: *said,* for *said,..*

6   M: *friend! This* for *friend: this*

7   M: *To come & touch my hand!..a simple thing*

    B: *To come and touch my hand..a simple thing,..*

8   M: *Yet I wept for it. This..the paper's light...*

    B: *Yet I wept for it!—This,...the paper's light,...*

9   M: *Said 'Dear I love the'!—and I sank & quailed*

    B: *Said, Dear, I love thee!—and I sank & quailed*

    H: *thee:* for *thee;*

    1850:   As in H

10 M: *gathered on* cancelled

         straight absorbed written above and cancelled

         past! for *past.*

    B: *past:* for *past.*

    H: As in B

    1850:   As in B

    1852:   As in B

11 M: *This said 'I am thine'! and so its ink has paled*

    B: *This said 'I am thine'—and so, its ink has paled*

12	M:	*of passionate beat* written above uncancelled end of line
	B:	*fast:* for *fast,*
	H:	As in B
	1850:	As in B
	1853:	As in B
13	M:	*And this . . . . ! O Love, thy words have ill availed,*
		& this . . and *have failed* written above
	B:	*this . . . . .* for *this . . .*
14	M:	*If what this said, I dare repeat at last.*
		my lips should dare repeat over uncancelled end of line

XXIX

1 I think of thee!—my thoughts do twine and bud
2 About thee, as wild vines, about a tree,
3 Put out broad leaves, and soon there's nought to see
4 Except the straggling green which hides the wood.
5 Yet, O my palm-tree, be it understood
6 I will not have my thoughts instead of thee
7 Who art dearer, better! rather instantly
8 Renew thy presence. As a strong tree should,
9 Rustle thy boughs and set thy trunk all bare,
10 And let these bands of greenery which insphere thee,
11 Drop heavily down, . . burst, shattered, everywhere!
12 Because, in this deep joy to see and hear thee
13 And breathe within thy shadow a new air,
14 I do not think of thee—I am too near thee.

5   The image of the palm plays a prominent role in the correspondence and is used in Sonnet XVII as well.

Heading

B: *Sonnet XXX*

    33 at upper right

H: *Sonnets from the Portuguese.*

H: *Thought and sight* cancelled (R)

XXIX

1   B: *I think of thee! my thoughts do twine & bud*

    H: *thee! for thee!—*

2   B: *About thee, as wild vines about a tree,—*

         vines about written over *briars around* erased (R)

    H: As in B

    1850:   As in B

    1853:   *About thee, as wild vines about a tree*

3   B: *Put out broad leaves,—and soon there's nought to see,*

5   B: *palm tree,* for *palm-tree,*

7   B: Upper case *R* in *rather*

    H: As in B

    1850:   As in B

    1853:   As in B

8   B: *presence!* for *presence.*

    H: As in B

    1850:   As in B

    1853:   As in B

9   B: *boughs,* for *boughs*

    H: As in B

    1850:   As in B

12 B: *&* for *and*

14 B: *I do not think of thee . . . I am too near thee!*

XXX

1 I see thine image through my tears to-night,
2 And yet to-day I saw thee smiling. How
3 Refer the cause?—Belovèd, is it thou
4 Or I? who makes me sad? The acolyte
5 Amid the chanted joy and thankful rite,
6 May so fall flat, with pale insensate brow,
7 On the altar-stair. I hear thy voice and vow
8 Perplexed, uncertain, since thou art out of sight,
9 As he, in his swooning ears, the choir's amen.
10 Belovèd, dost thou love? or did I see all
11 The glory as I dreamed, and fainted when
12 Too vehement light dilated my ideal,
13 For my soul's eyes? Will that light come again,
14 As now these tears come . . . falling hot and real?

Heading

B: *Sonnet XXXI*

    34 at upper right

H: *Sonnets from the Portuguese.*

    XXX

1	B:	*to night,* for *to-night,*
	H:	As in B
2	B:	*And yet today I saw thee smiling. How,*
	H:	*today* for *to-day*
3	B:	*Refer the cause? Beloved, is it thou*
	H:	*Beloved,* for *Belovèd,*
	1850:	As in H
	1853:	As in H
4	B:	*I? . . for I?*
5	B:	*& solemn rite,*
6	B:	*May, so,* for *May so*
7	B:	*&* for *and*
8	B:	*Perplexed., uncertain., since thou'rt out of sight,*
		The commas following the periods had been periods
	H:	*thou'rt* for *thou art*
	1850:	As in H
	1853:	As in H
9	B:	*amen!* for *amen.*
	H:	As in B
	1850:	As in B
	1853:	As in B
10	B:	*Beloved, dost thou love?, . . or did I see all*
		me cancelled after *love*
		did written over *have* erased
	H:	*Beloved,* for *Belovèd,*

10	1850:	As in H
	1853:	As in H
12	B:	*Ideal,* for *ideal,*
	H:	*ideal* for *ideal,*
	1850:	As in H
	1853:	As in H
14	B:	*As now these tears come, ... falling hot and real?*
		come written over erased *coming*

XXXI

1 Thou comest! all is said without a word.
2 I sit beneath thy looks, as children do
3 In the noon-sun, with souls that tremble through
4 Their happy eyelids from an unaverred
5 Yet prodigal inward joy. Behold, I erred
6 In that last doubt! and yet I cannot rue
7 The sin most, but the occasion . . . that we two
8 Should for a moment stand unministered
9 By a mutual presence. Ah, keep near and close,
10 Thou dovelike help! and, when my fears would rise,
11 With thy broad heart serenely interpose.
12 Brood down with thy divine sufficiencies
13 These thoughts which tremble when bereft of those,
14 Like callow birds left desert to the skies.

Heading

B: *Sonnet XXXII*

    35 at upper right

H: *Sonnets from the Portuguese.*

    XXXI

1	B:	*word!* for *word.*
4	B:	*eyelids,* for *eyelids*
6	B:	*And* for *and*
7	B:	*occasion....* for *occasion...*
8	B:	*unministerred* for *unministered*
9	B:	*&* for *and*
10	B:	*Thou dovelike soul! and when my fears would rise,*
		Thou written above cancelled *My*
	H:	*help* written over erased word
11	B:	*interpose!* for *interpose.*
	H:	As in B
		heart written over erased *breast* (?)
	1850:	As in B
	1853:	As in B
13	B:	*those,—* for *those,*

XXXII

1 The first time that the sun rose on thine oath
2 To love me, I looked forward to the moon
3 To slacken all those bonds which seemed too soon
4 And quickly tied to make a lasting troth.
5 Quick-loving hearts, I thought, may quickly loathe;
6 And, looking on myself, I seemed not one
7 For such man's love!—more like an out of tune
8 Worn viol, a good singer would be wroth
9 To spoil his song with, and which, snatched in haste,
10 Is laid down at the first ill-sounding note.
11 I did not wrong myself so, but I placed
12 A wrong on *thee*. For perfect strains may float
13 'Neath master-hands, from instruments defaced,—
14 And great souls, at one stroke, may do and doat.

The theme of this sonnet is repeated, with a variation, in Sonnet XXXVI.

Heading

B: *Sonnet XXXIII*

    36 at upper right

H: *Sonnets from the Portuguese*

H: XXXII

4	B:	*troth* written over *oath* (R)
5	B:	*loathe.* for *loathe;*
8	H:	*wroth* written over *loath* erased
9	B:	*with;* for *with,*
12	B:	*float,* for *float*
13	B:	*defaced,..* for *defaced,–*
14	B:	& for second *and*

XXXIII

1 Yes, call me by my pet-name! let me hear
2 The name I used to run at, when a child,
3 From innocent play, and leave the cowslips piled,
4 To glance up in some face that proved me dear
5 With the look of its eyes. I miss the clear
6 Fond voices, which, being drawn and reconciled
7 Into the music of Heaven's undefiled,
8 Call me no longer. Silence on the bier,
9 While I call God . . call God!—So let thy mouth
10 Be heir to those who are now exanimate.
11 Gather the north flowers to complete the south,
12 And catch the early love up in the late.
13 Yes, call me by that name,—and I, in truth,
14 With the same heart, will answer, and not wait.

In his letter of December 19, 1845, Browning called E.B.B. "Ba" for the first time, having failed in the attempt when he saw her in person a few days before.

5-8 The voices referred to probably belonged to E.B.B.'s mother, her brother Edward, her favorite in the family, her sister Maria, perhaps even her uncle Samuel with whom she was very close and who had left her financially independent.

Heading

B: *Sonnet XXXIV*

    38 at upper right

H: *Sonnets from the Portuguese.*

    XXXIII

    Old names— cancelled

1   B: *me* written over *her*

2   B: *sound* for *name*

3   B: *&* for *and*

    drop cancelled and *leave* written above

4   B: *look* for *glance*

   1853:   *So* for *To*

5   B: second *the* cancelled and *some* written above

6   B: *&* for *and*

8   B: ME for *me*

9   H: *I* for *I*

   1850:   As in H

10 B: *exanimate!* for *exanimate.*

   H: *exanimate:* for *exanimate.*

   1850:   As in H

   1853:   As in H

11 B: *north-flowers* for *north flowers*

   H: As in B

12 B: *late!* for *late.*

12	H:	As in B
	1850:	As in B
	1853:	As in B
13	B:	*name*— for *name*,—
14	B:	*will answer & not wait.*

XXXIV

1 With the same heart, I said, I'll answer thee
2 As those, when thou shalt call me by my name—
3 Lo, the vain promise! is the same, the same,
4 Perplexed and ruffled by life's strategy?
5 When called before, I told how hastily
6 I dropped my flowers or brake off from a game,
7 To run and answer with the smile that came
8 At play last moment, and went on with me
9 Through my obedience. When I answer now,
10 I drop a grave thought,—break from solitude;—
11 Yet still my heart goes to thee . . . ponder how . .
12 Not as to a single good, but all my good!
13 Lay thy hand on it, best one, and allow
14 That no child's foot could run fast as this blood.

Heading

B: *Sonnet XXXV*

   39 at upper right

H: *Sonnets from the Portuguese.*

   XXXIV

H: *Old names*
             both cancelled
     CONTINUED

     The compositor's name, *Richardson*, at upper left

 2   B: *name!* for *name—*

 3   B: *Lo the vain promise! Is the same the same*

 4   B: *Perplexed & ruffled by Life's strategy?* with *all* cancelled and
          written above cancelled line *If vexed by years and worn by
          memory?* (R)

 5   B: *have* before *told* cancelled

          certainly for *hastily*

 6   B: *flowers,* for *flowers*

     H: As in B

     1850:   As in B

     1853:   *game* for *game,*

10   B: *I drop a sad thought, . . break from solitude—*

     H: *I drop a grave thought;—break from solitude:—*

     1850:   As in B

11   B: *Yet my heart goes to thee, . . consider how . .*

          consider written over *remember*

     H: *my* cancelled between *yet* and *still*

12   B: *Not as to good, but as to all my good!*

          one cancelled between *to* and *good*

     H: *good* for first *good,*

          a single written above cancelled *one*

          to cancelled between *but* and *all*

12   1850:   As in H

     1853:   As in H

13   B: *Lay thy hand on it, best One! . . & allow*

XXXV

1 If I leave all for thee, wilt thou exchange
2 And be all to me? Shall I never miss
3 Home-talk and blessing and the common kiss
4 That comes to each in turn, nor count it strange,
5 When I look up, to drop on a new range
6 Of walls and floors . . another home than this?
7 Nay, wilt thou fill that place by me which is
8 Filled by dead eyes too tender to know change?
9 That's hardest. If to conquer love, has tried,
10 To conquer grief, tries more . . . as all things prove;
11 For grief indeed is love and grief beside.
12 Alas, I have grieved so I am hard to love.
13 Yet love me—wilt thou? Open thine heart wide,
14 And fold within, the wet wings of thy dove.

Heading

B: *Sonnet XXXVI*

    40 at upper right

H: *Sonnets from the Portuguese.* with *the* written over *thy*

    XXXV

1 B: *If I leave all for <u>thee,</u> wilt thou exchange,*

2   B: *be*

    H: As in B

    1850:   *be* italicized

    1853:   As in 1850

3   H: *blessing,* for *blessing*

    H: As in B

    1850:   As in B

4   B: *Which comes to each in turn?.. nor count it strange*

         to each in turn is written above heavily cancelled words

6   B: *&* for *and*

7   B: *Nay* written over *And* cancelled and restored in the margin

8   B: *change?* with the question mark added in darker ink after ;—
         and intended to replace it

    H: *eyes,* for *eyes*

    1850:   As in H

9   B: *That's hardest! If to conquer Love has tried,..*

         If written over *As*

    H: *hardest!* for *hardest.*

    1850:   As in H

    1853:   *That's hardest! If to conquer love has tried,*

10 B: *To conquer grief, tries more;—as all things prove!*

         The original line is erased and the last six words are written
         above heavy cancellations

    H: *To conquer grief tries more ... as all things prove:*

    1850:   As in H

    1853:   *grief* for *grief,*

11 B: *For Grief indeed is Love . . . and grief beside!*

    H: *love,* for *love*

    1850:   As in H

12 B: *Alas! I have grieved so, I am hard to love—*

    H: *love—* for *love.*

    1850:   As in H

    1853:   As in H

14 1853:   *within* for *within,*

XXXVI

1 When we met first and loved, I did not build
2 Upon the event with marble. Could it mean
3 To last, a love set pendulous between
4 Sorrow and sorrow? Nay, I rather thrilled,
5 Distrusting every light that seemed to gild
6 The onward path, and feared to overlean
7 A finger even. And, though I have grown serene
8 And strong since then, I think that God has willed
9 A still renewable fear . . O love, O troth . .
10 Lest these enclaspèd hands should never hold,
11 This mutual kiss drop down between us both
12 As an unowned thing, once the lips being cold.
13 And Love, be false! if *he*, to keep one oath,
14 Must lose one joy, by his life's star foretold.

Cf. Sonnet XXXII.

Heading

B: *Sonnet XXXVII*

    42 at upper right

H: *Sonnets from the Portuguese.*

H: XXXVI

1   B: & for *and*

4   B: & for *and*

6   B: & for *and*

7   B: *And* for *And,*

    H: As in B

9   B: *o love, o troth, . .*

    H: lower case *o* both times

10 B: *Lest these enclasped hands should never hold . .*

    H: *enclasped* for *enclaspèd*

    1850:   As in H

    1853:   As in H

11 B: *both,* for *both*

12 B: *cold!* for *cold.*

13 B: *And, Love, be false! if* HE, *to keep one oath,*

         the cancelled and *one* written above

    H: *Love* for *Love,*

    1850:   As in H

    1853:   As in H

14 B: *Must lose one joy by his star of life foretold.*

    H: *joy* for *joy,*

    1850:   As in H

    1853:   As in H

XXXVII

1 Pardon, oh, pardon, that my soul should make
2 Of all that strong divineness which I know
3 For thine and thee, an image only so
4 Formed of the sand, and fit to shift and break.
5 It is that distant years which did not take
6 Thy sovranty, recoiling with a blow,
7 Have forced my swimming brain to undergo
8 Their doubt and dread, and blindly to forsake
9 Thy purity of likeness, and distort
10 Thy worthiest love to a worthless counterfeit.
11 As if a shipwrecked Pagan, safe in port,
12 His guardian sea-god to commemorate,
13 Should set a sculptured porpoise, gills a-snort,
14 And vibrant tail, within the temple-gate.

9-14 According to Porter and Clarke this is an allusion to the custom of commemorating the god who has saved one with a statue which, inevitably, can only be a weak echo of the god's divine qualities.

Heading

B: *Sonnet XXXVIII*

43 at upper right

H: *Sonnets from the Portuguese*

   XXXVII

3   B: & for *and*

4   B: & for each *and*

5   B: *is,* for *is*

8   B: & for first *and*

9   B: *likeness* for *likeness,*

10   B: *Thy worthiest love with worthless counterfeit!*

     H: *Thy worthiest love with worthless counterfeit.*

     1850:   As in H

     1853:   As in H

11   B: lower case *p* in *Pagan*

     H: As in B

12   B: *seagod* for *sea-god*

13   B: *porpoise . . .* for *porpoise,*

14   B: *tail, ...* for *tail,*

XXXVIII

1 First time he kissed me, he but only kissed
2 The fingers of this hand wherewith I write;
3 And, ever since, it grew more clean and white, . .
4 Slow to world-greetings . . quick with its 'Oh, list,'
5 When the angels speak. A ring of amethyst
6 I could not wear here, plainer to my sight,
7 Than that first kiss. The second passed in height
8 The first, and sought the forehead, and half missed,
9 Half falling on the hair. O beyond meed!
10 That was the chrism of love, which love's own crown,
11 With sanctifying sweetness, did precede.
12 The third upon my lips was folded down
13 In perfect, purple state; since when, indeed,
14 I have been proud and said, 'My love, my own.'

5-6 The use of the gem here is similar to that of Sonnet XII which originally derived from Browning's metaphor for E.B.B.'s love for her brother Edward.

Heading

B: *Sonnet XXXIX*

    44 at upper right

Sonnets from the Portuguese

H: *Sonnets from the Portuguese*

XXXVIII

2   B: *write,* for *write;*

       H: As in B

       1850:   As in B

       1853:   As in B

3   B: *And ever since it grew more clean & white . .*

       H: *And ever since it grew more clean and white, . .*

       1850:   As in H

       1853:   As in H

4   B: *"Oh, list"* for *'Oh, list,'*

       1850:   Double quotations marks

5   B: *When the angels spake. A ring of amethyst,*

6   B: *here* for *here,*

       H: As in B

       1850:   As in B

       1853:   As in B

7   B: *kiss!—* for *kiss.*

          than written over *that*

          height written over another word

8   B: *&* for each *and*

9   B: *Half falling on the hair.—Oh, Beyond meed!*

          Originally *Beyond my meed!* with *my* cancelled and *Oh* inserted to give final reading

       H: *hair . .* for *hair.*

10	B:	*That was the chrism of Love, which, Love's own crown,*
11	B:	*precede!* for *precede.*
12	B:	*The third, upon my lips, was folded down,*
	H:	*The third, upon my lips, was folded down*
	1850:	As in H
13	B:	*state!* for *state;*
	H:	As in B
	1850:	As in B
	1853:	As in B
14	B:	*I have been proud, and said, . . "My Love, my own."*
	H:	Upper case *l* in *love*
	1850:	As in H
		Double quotation marks

XXXIX

1 Because thou hast the power and own'st the grace
2 To look through and behind this mask of me,
3 (Against which years have beat thus blanchingly
4 With their rains,) and behold my soul's true face,
5 The dim and weary witness of life's race!—
6 Because thou has the faith and love to see,
7 Through that same soul's distracting lethargy,
8 The patient angel waiting for a place
9 In the new Heavens!—because nor sin nor woe,
10 Nor God's infliction, nor death's neighbourhood,
11 Nor all which others viewing, turn to go, . .
12 Nor all which makes me tired of all, self-viewed, . .
13 Nothing repels thee, . . Dearest, teach me so
14 To pour out gratitude, as thou dost, good.

Heading

B: *Sonnet XL*

   45 at upper right

H: *Sonnets from the Portuguese.*

   XXXIX

   The compositor's name, *Flose,* at upper left

1	B:	& for *and*
2	B:	& for *and*
3	B:	(Against which, years have beat thus blenchingly
	H:	As in B
	1850:	As in B
	1853:	which, for *which*
4	B:	With their rains!) and behold my Soul's true face ..
	H:	rains! for *rains,)*
	1850:	As in H
	1853:	As in H
5	B:	The dim and weary witness of Life's race!
	H:	race:— for *race!—*
	1850:	As in H
	1853:	race,— for *race!—*
6	B:	see for *see,*
8	B:	his for *a*
		Last reading written over erased line the last part of which reads *nor woe*
	H:	As in B
	1850:	As in B
9	B:	In the new Heavens. Because nor sin, nor woe,
	H:	In the new Heavens:—because nor sin nor woe
	1850:	Heavens: for *Heavens!—*
	1853:	Heavens,— for *Heavens!—*
11	B:	which, for *which*
	H:	all, for *all*

11	1850:	As in H
12	B:	*selfviewed,..* for *self-viewed,..*
	H:	As in B
13	B:	*.. Nothing repels thee .. Dearest, teach me so*
		Upper case written over lower *d*
14	H:	*good!* for *good.*
	1850:	As in H
	1853:	As in H

XL

1 Oh, yes! they love through all this world of ours!

2 I will not gainsay love, called love forsooth.

3 I have heard love talked in my early youth,

4 And since, not so long back but that the flowers

5 Then gathered, smell still. Mussulmans and Giaours

6 Throw kerchiefs at a smile, and have no ruth

7 For any weeping. Polypheme's white tooth

8 Slips on the nut, if, after frequent showers,

9 The shell is over-smooth,—and not so much

10 Will turn the thing called love, aside to hate,

11 Or else to oblivion. But thou art not such

12 A lover, my Belovèd! thou canst wait

13 Through sorrow and sickness, to bring souls to touch,

14 And think it soon when others cry 'Too late.'

---

1   Sonnet XL expresses Elizabeth's characteristic skepticism about love, "called love forsooth," which she explained to Browning for the first time on December 12, 1845:

> It is true of me . . very true . . that I have not a high appreciation of what passes in the world [. . .] under the name of love; & that a distrust of the thing had grown to be a habit of mind with me when I knew you first.
> (I, 340)

With characteristic perceptiveness, she went on to say that the reasons for her skepticism are not merely the fact that men and women do sometimes deliberately deceive each other, but also that most people and even the best of people very frequently deceive themselves about the nature of their own feelings and about the characters and qualities of those whom they love. While she never doubted Browning's integrity and sincerity, Elizabeth repeatedly expressed the fear that he was mistaking a compassionate chivalry for love in his feelings for her. She was also uneasy about his generous estimate of her as a writer.

5   *Giaours*—a disparaging term used by the Turks for Christians and other infidels. The suggestion is that all men are attracted to gayety and have no pity for sadness, in contrast to Browning who has the pity and patience—lines 11 through 14—to go beyond grief, to wait out the erosion of habitual sorrow. The theme is repeated in Sonnets XXV, XXVII, XXXII, XXXIX.

7   This is a somewhat mystifying image explained by Porter and Clarke in this way: "Polyphemus, the Cyclops, one-eyed giant son of Neptune, who was in love with Galatea, the sea-nymph, in a crude and petulant way; but she, scoffing at his one eye and shaggy eyebrow, escaped him, hence the image of the white tooth of his appetite slipping on the coveted kernel." (III, 400.) This explanation doesn't seem altogether satisfactory since it does not account for the "frequent showers" of line 8. Showers and rain usually symbolize sorrow and pain in E.B.B.'s poetry, and I think we can assume that she is here referring to Galatea's sorrow at the death of Acis, whom Polyphemus killed—in one version of the story—and with him all possibility of love from Galatea. In another version of the story Galatea and Polyphemus were married.

Heading

B: *XLI*

    46 at upper right

H: *Sonnets from the Portuguese.*

    XL

1   B: *Oh yes! they love through all this world of ours!* . . (?)

2   B: *forsooth!* for *forsooth.*

3   B: *dawning* for *early*

A Variorum Edition 141

5   B: *Then gathered, smell still! Mussulmans & Giaours*

6   B: *&* for *and*

7   B: *weeping!* for *weeping.*

8   B: *Slips on the nut, if after frequent showers*

       H: As in B

       1850:   As in B

       1853:   As in B

9   B: *The shell is oversmooth, and not so much*

            Cancelled punctuation and letter after *oversmooth*

       H: *oversmooth;* for *over-smooth,—*

       1850:   *over-smooth;* for *over-smooth,—*

10   1853:   *hate* for *hate,*

11   B: *Or else to oblivion! But <u>thou</u> art not such*

12   B: *A lover, my beloved! <u>thou</u> canst wait*

       H: *beloved!* for *Belovèd!*

       1850:   *Beloved!* for *Belovèd!*

       1853:   As in 1850

13   B: *Through sorrow & sickness, to bring souls to touch,..*

            sickness written over *shame*

            two cancelled before *bring* and *souls*

14   1850:   Double quotation marks

XLI

1 I thank all who have loved me in their hearts,
2 With thanks and love from mine. Deep thanks to all
3 Who paused a little near the prison-wall,
4 To hear my music in its louder parts,
5 Ere they went onward, each one to the mart's
6 Or temple's occupation, beyond call.
7 But thou, who, in my voice's sink and fall,
8 When the sob took it, thy divinest Art's
9 Own instrument didst drop down at thy foot,
10 To harken what I said between my tears, . .
11 Instruct me how to thank thee!—Oh, to shoot
12 My soul's full meaning into future years,
13 That *they* should lend it utterance, and salute
14 Love that endures, from Life that disappears!

Heading

B: *XLII*

    47 at upper right

H: *Sonnets from the Portuguese.*

    XLI

2   B: *Or thought they did so!* cancelled and *With thanks and love from mine! Deep* written above it

        Andreas Mayor assumes that the cancelled line is an allusion to the jealous love Elizabeth's father had for his family and commends E.B.B.'s generosity in cancelling even so mild a reproach. (*Sonnets from the Portuguese and Seven Other Poems* [Utrecht: De Roos, 1957].)

3   B: *the* written over *my*

       prison-wall for *prison-wall,*

    H: As in B

4   B: *my* written over *the*

5   B: *one,* for *one*

6   B: *Expectant* cancelled (R) and *Or temple's* written above

7   B: <u>*thou*</u>

       But written above cancelled word

    H: *who* for *who,*

    1850:   As in H

    1853:   As in H

8   B: *When the sob caught it, . . . thy divinest Art's*

9   B: *instrument,* for *instrument*

    H: As in B

    1850:   As in B

10   B: *tears, ...* for *tears, . .*

11   B: *THEE!—* for *thee!—*

12   B: Exclamation point after *years* changed to comma and dash

13   1853:   *utterance* for *utterance,*

14   B: *with* for *from*

    H: As in B

14   1850:   As in B
     1853:   As in B

XLII

1 *'My future will not copy fair my past'*—
2 I wrote that once; and thinking at my side
3 My ministering life-angel justified
4 The word by his appealing look upcast
5 To the white throne of God, I turned at last,
6 And there, instead, saw thee, not unallied
7 To angels in thy soul! Then I, long tried
8 By natural ills, received the comfort fast,
9 While budding, at thy sight, my pilgrim's staff
10 Gave out green leaves with morning dews impearled.
11 I seek no copy now of life's first half:
12 Leave here the pages with long musing curled,
13 And write me new my future's epigraph,
14 New angel mine, unhoped for in the world!

XLII is a reversal of "Past and Future," a Sonnet which Browning read in *Poems*, 1844. On November 16, 1845, he wrote to Elizabeth "I have been reading among other poems that sonnet—"Past and Future"—which affects me more than any poem I ever read" (I, 273). Kintner, in his note to Browning's letter, feels that there is surely a connection between this reference to it and Sonnet XLII. This is further supported by the fact that the Sonnet was originally XVII in the sequence.

Sonnets from the Portuguese

Heading

B: *Sonnet XVII*

> This sonnet was probably number XVII, now missing, in the Morgan sequence. The correspondence indicates that it was probably composed towards the end of November, 1845, just before the two sonnets, XVIII and XIX, dealing with the exchange of locks of hair. It was taken out of the sequence for the printer's copy, the Houghton MS, and appeared in 1850 and in 1853 on page 362 of Volume I as an independent sonnet entitled "Future and Past." In 1856 it was restored to the sequence, but as number XLII, not XVII. Number XLII and XLIII of the Houghton MS and the editions of 1850 and 1853 became XLIII and XLIV in 1856 and all subsequent editions.

1   B: *"My future will not copy fair my past.."*

      1850:   *My future will not copy fair my past.* in italics

      1853:   As in 1850

2   1850:   *and,* for *and*

      1853:   As in 1850

4   B: *The words by his appealing looks upcast*

          My cancelled and *The* written above

6   B: *And saw thee here instead o thou allied*

          there cancelled and *here* written above

      1850:   *And saw instead there, thee; not unallied* with *thee* italicized

      1853:   *And saw instead there, thee,—not unallied* with *thee* italicized

7   B: *To angels in thy soul, though not untried* (R) cancelled, erased and overwritten to read as in 1856, with the last five words written above

8   B: *By natural ills, received the comfort fast;*

          Last four words written above cancelled *My heart beat wild and fast*

9   B: *While* cancelled for *And* above the line

9   B: *While* restored

    1850:   *budding* for *budding,*

    1853:   As in 1850

10 B: *Gave out green leaves with morning-dew impearled!*

    1853:   No punctuation visible after *impearled*

11 B: *half . .* for *half:*

       Seek me written in pencil above *I seek*

       now written above cancelled *even*

       first cancelled with *early* written above, cancelled and *first* restored above it

    1850:   *—I seek no copy now of life's first half!*

    1853:   As in 1850

12 B: *Leave there, the pages with long musing curled!* written above line over pencilled words

       The original read *The blots will be there on the pages curled!* (R) cancelled except for *curled!*

    1853:   *curled,—* for *curled,*

13 B: *And* written above cancelled *Come*

XLIII

1 How do I love thee? Let me count the ways.

2 I love thee to the depth and breadth and height

3 My soul can reach, when feeling out of sight

4 For the ends of Being and ideal Grace.

5 I love thee to the level of everyday's

6 Most quiet need, by sun and candelight.

7 I love thee freely, as men strive for Right;

8 I love thee purely, as they turn from Praise.

9 I love thee with the passion put to use

10 In my old griefs, and with my childhood's faith.

11 I love thee with a love I seemed to lose

12 With my lost saints,—I love thee with the breath,

13 Smiles, tears, of all my life!—and, if God choose,

14 I shall but love thee better after death.

    Sonnet XLIII is the only triumphant declaration of love. William Andrews Clark suggests that it is patterned after Goneril's speech to Lear. This is quite possible since both the Brownings knew Shakespeare very well —the letters have dozens of Shakespearean allusions from both correspondents—but that it was a conscious echo is highly unlikely. Elizabeth would not consciously have written her triumphant song of love along the lines of the disloyal, hypocritical Goneril's:

    Sir, I love you more than words can wield the matter;
    Dearer than eye-sight, space, and liberty;
    Beyond what can be valued, rich or rare;
    No less than life, with grace, health, beauty, honour;
    As much as child e'er loved, or father found;
    A love that makes breath poor and speech unable;

Beyond all manner of so much I love you.

(*Lear*, I, i)

As an unconscious inspiration to memory and imagination, the speech is a possible pattern for the poem. The poem's well-known lines also find an echo in Mrs. Browning's *Aurora Leigh:*

Thus, 't was granted me
To know he loved me to the depth and height
Of such large natures,

(IX, ll. 752-4)

Heading

B: *XLIII*

   49 at upper right

H: *XLII*

   A Confession or *A Profession.* cancelled

   Since the Houghton MS was the printer's copy for the 1850 edition in which Sonnet XLII was printed outside of the sequence, this Sonnet is numbered XLII and remained XLII until the 1856 edition.

   XLIII pencilled at upper right in a different hand

1   B: *ways!* for *ways.*

2   B: & for each *and*

4   B: Upper case *I* in *ideal*

   H: As in B

   1850:   As in B

   1853:   As in B

6   B: & for *and*

7   B: *Right,—* for *Right;*

A Variorum Edition 153

8 B: *Praise,!.* for *Praise.*

  H: *Praise:* for *Praise.*

  1850: *Praise;* for *Praise.*

  1853: As in 1850

9 B: *passion,* written over *passionate*

10 B: *In my old griefs, . . and with my childhood's faith!*

   my childhood's written above cancelled the *child's old*

  H: *faith:* for *faith.*

  1850: *faith;* for *faith.*

  1853: As in 1850

11 B: *the* for *a*

  H: As in B

12 B: *Saints!* written over illegible word

  H: *saints!* for *saints,—*

14 B: *my* cancelled before *death*

XLIV

1 Belovèd, thou hast brought me many flowers
2 Plucked in the garden, all the summer through
3 And winter, and it seemed as if they grew
4 In this close room, nor missed the sun and showers.
5 So, in the like name of that love of ours,
6 Take back these thoughts which here unfolded too,
7 And which on warm and cold days I withdrew
8 From my heart's ground. Indeed, those beds and bowers
9 Be overgrown with bitter weeds and rue,
10 And wait thy weeding; yet there's eglantine,
11 Here's ivy!—take them, as I used to do
12 Thy flowers, and keep them where they shall not pine.
13 Instruct thine eyes to keep the colours true,
14 And tell thy soul, their roots are left in mine.

The final sonnet celebrates his gift of flowers, symbolic of his love, and offers the wreath of sonnts in return. Browning brought flowers as long as they were available, usually from his mother's garden, and surprisingly long into the winter and very early in the spring. Throughout the correspondence Elizabeth thanked Browning repeatedly for the flowers. One example, from a letter written on December 30, 1845, shows her delight, gratitude and wonder:

When you are gone I find your flowers; & you never spoke of nor showed them to me—so instead of yesterday I thank you to-day —thank you. Count them among the miracles that your flowers live with me—I accept *that* for an omen, dear—dearest! Flowers in general, all other flowers, die of despair when they come into the same atmosphere . . used to do it so constantly & observably that it made me melancholy & I left off for the most part having them here. Now, you see how they put up with the close room, & condescend to me & the dust—it is true and no fancy!

(I, 348)

Kintner, in a note, quotes from a letter of Elizabeth's to Mrs. Martin, written in 1843, in which she laments the fact that flowers die quickly in her room.

E.B.B.'s letters frequently mention Browning's flowers to her, her gratitude, her astonishment at the fact that they seemed to thrive in her close room where she could not keep flowers and plants alive for long before his.

8-12 On July 16, 1846, E.B.B. used the same image of weeds and flowers intertwined, in another context. She told Browning that if her father had been closer to her and warmer, he would have been in her confidence from the beginning and would have stopped their courtship long before it became that. "So the nightshade & eglantine are twisted, twined, one in the other, . . & the little pink roses lean up against the pale poison of the berries—we cannot tear this from that, let us think of it ever so much!" she concluded. (II, 882.)

Heading

B: *XLIV*

    50 at upper right

H: *Sonnets from the Portuguese.*

    XLIII

1   B: *Beloved,* for *Belovèd,*

    H: As in B

    1850: As in B

    1853: As in B

2   B: *Plucked in the garden all the summer through,*

3	B:	*winter;* for *winter,*
4	B:	*&* for *and*
	1853:	*room* for *room,*
6	B:	*Take back these thoughts, which here, unfolded, too,*
	H:	*thoughts,* for *thoughts*
	1850:	As in H
7	B:	*&* for second *and*
	H:	As in B
8	B:	*From my heart's ground. Indeed those beds & bowers*
		Indeed written above pencilled out *And of*
		Parenthesis before *Indeed*
9	B:	*Be overgrown with bitter weeds & rue*
10	B:	*eglantine—* for *eglantine,*
		Yet here's written above heavy cancellation
	H:	*And wait thy weeding: yet here's eglantine,*
	1850:	As in H
11	B:	*Here's ivy!)—take them, as I used to do*
		Here's ivy! written above cancelled *Springs wildly*
12	B:	*pine!* for *pine.*
	H:	*pine:* for *pine.*
	1850:	As in H
	1853:	*pine;* for *pine.*
14	B:	*are* written over *were*

At lower right corner in E.B.B.'s hand

50 Wimpole Street

1846, Sept.

───

Married—September 12th,

───

1846.

──

Appendix

The following appendix lists the unauthorized changes between the Houghton MS, the printer's copy, and the edition of *Poems,* 1850, and records the subsequent fate of those changes. In Sonnet VII, for example, the Houghton MS has "Sweet", which appears in 1850 as "sweet". The change to lower case in 1850 is retained in 1853, but restored to upper case in 1856.

Sonnets from the Portuguese

	Houghton MS	1850	1853	1856
I.	single quotation marks	double quotation marks	single	single
	'Death'!	"Death!"	changed retained, single qu. m.	retained
II.	single qu. m.	double qu. m.	single	single
III.	*destinies*.	*destinies* . . (could be paper)	restored	restored
V.	*bead*	*bead,*	retained	retained
	my	*My*	restored	restored
VI.	*forbore,* . . .	*forbore,* . .	retained	retained
VII.	*Sweet*	*sweet*	retained	retained
VIII.	*take*	*take,*	restored	restored
	cold! (ambiguous)	*cold!—*	retained	*cold,—*
IX.	*smiles*	*smiles,*	restored	restored
X.	*love* (gram. error)	*love,*	retained	retained
XI.	*music!* . . .	*music!* . .	retained	*music,—*
	beloved	*Beloved*	retained	retained

Appendix

	Houghton MS	1850	1853	1856
XIV.	single qu. m.	double	single	single
XVI.	single qu. m.	double	single	single
XVIII.	May cry	May cry,	retained	changed altogether
XVIII.	single qu. m.	double	single	single
XIX.	counterpart,...	counterpart,...	retained	retained
XX.	heart,	heart	retained	restored
XX.	beloved	Beloved	retained	retained
XXI.	single qu. m.	double	single	single
XXII.	me——	me—	retained	retained
XXII.	their	the	retained	retained
XXII.	deathhour	death-hour	retained	retained
XXIII.	beloved	Beloved	retained	Belovèd
XXVII.	beloved	Beloved	retained	Belovèd
XXVIII.	tonight	to-night	retained	retained

	Houghton MS	1850	1853	1856
XXIX.	*thee!*	*thee!—*	retained	retained
XXXIII.	*north-flowers*	*north flowers*	retained	retained
XXXVI.	*And*	*And,*	retained	retained
	o (twice)	*O* (twice)	retained	retained
XXXVII.	*pagan*	*Pagan*	retained	retained
XXXVIII.	single qu. m.	double	single	single
	hair ..	*hair.*	retained	retained
XXXIX.	*Heavens:—*	*Heavens:*	*Heavens,—*	*Heavens!—*
	woe	*woe,*	retained	retained
XL.	*oversmooth;*	*over-smooth;*	*over-smooth,—*	As in 1853
	beloved!	*Beloved!*	retained	*Belovèd!*
	single qu. m.	double	single	single
XLI.	*prison-wall*	*prison-wall,*	retained	retained
XLIII.	*faith:*	*faith;*	retained	*faith.*

Appendix

Houghton MS		1850	1853	1856
XLIII.	*the*	*a*	retained	retained
	saints!	*saints,—*	retained	retained
XLIV.	*&*	*and*	retained	retained

BIBLIOGRAPHY

A. Mrs. Browning's Works

I. Poetry and Diary

Aurora Leigh and Other Poems. Introduced by Cora Kaplan. London: The Women's Press, 1978.

Casa Guidi Windows. Ed. Julia Markus. New York: The Browning Institute, 1977.

The Complete Works of Elizabeth Barrett Browning. Eds. Charlotte Porter and Helen Clarke. 6 vols. 1900; rpt. New York: AMS Press Inc., 1973.

The Poetical Works of Elizabeth Barrett Browning. With a new Introduction by Ruth M. Adams. Ed. Harriet Waters Preston. 1900; rpt. Boston: Houghton Mifflin, 1974.

Poems. 1st ed. 2 vols. London: Moxon, 1844.

Poems. 2nd ed. 2 vols. London: Chapman and Hall, 1850.

Poems. 3rd ed. 2 vols. London: Chapman and Hall, 1853.

Poems. 4th ed. 3 vols. London: Chapman and Hall, 1856.

Sonnets from the Portuguese. MS. Pierpont Morgan Library.

Sonnets from the Portuguese. MS. British Library, Additional Manuscript 43487.

Sonnets from the Portuguese. MS. Private Collection of Mr. Arthur Houghton, Jr.

Sonnets from the Portuguese. Ed. William Andrews Clark, Jr. San Francisco: Nash, 1927.

Sonnets from the Portuguese. Centennial Variorum Edition. Ed. Fannie Ratchford. New York: P. C. Duschenes, 1950.

Sonnets from the Portuguese and Seven Other Poems. Ed. Andreas Mayor. Utrecht: De Roos, 1957.

Sonnets from the Portuguese: A Facsimile Edition of the British Library Manuscript. Ed. William S. Peterson. Barre: Barre Publishing, 1977.

Diary by E. B. B. Eds. Philip Kelley and Ronald Hudson. Athens: Ohio University Press, 1969.

II. Letters

Letters of Elizabeth Barrett Browning Addressed to Richard Hengist Horne. Ed. S. R. Townshend Mayer. 2 vols. London: Richard Bentley, 1877.

The Letters of Elizabeth Barrett Browning. Ed. Frederic G. Kenyon. 2 vols. New York: Macmillan, 1897.

Elizabeth Barrett Browning: Letters to Her Sister, 1846-1859. Ed. Leonard Huxley. London: John Murray, 1929.

Elizabeth Barrett to Miss Mitford. Ed. Betty Miller. London: John Murray, 1954.

Elizabeth Barrett to Mr. Boyd. Ed. Barbara P. McCarthy. New Haven: Yale University Press for Wellesley College, 1955.

Letters of the Brownings to George Barrett. Eds. Paul Landis and Ronald E. Freeman. Urbana: University of Illinois Press, 1958.

The Letters of Robert Browning and Elizabeth Barrett Barrett 1845-1846. Ed. Elvan Kintner. Cambridge: The Belknap Press of Harvard University Press, 1969.

B. Biographies of Mrs. Browning

Burdett, Osbert. *The Brownings.* Boston: Houghton Mifflin Co., 1929.

Hayter, Alethea. *Mrs. Browning: A Poet's Work and Its Setting.* London: Faber and Faber, 1962.

Hewlett, Dorothy. *Elizabeth Barrett Browning.* New York: Knopf, 1952.

Marks, Jeannette. *The Family of the Barrett.* New York: Macmillan, 1938.

Taplin, Garner B. *The Life of Elizabeth Barrett Browning.* New Haven: Yale University Press, 1957.

Whiting, Lilian. *The Brownings: Their Life and Art.* Boston: Little Brown, 1911.

C. Letters of Robert Browning

Letters of Robert Browning Collected by Thomas J. Wise. Ed. Thurman L. Hood. London: John Murray, 1933.

Robert Browning and Julia Wedgwood. Ed. Richard Curle. New York: Fredric A. Stokes, 1937.

New Letters of Robert Browning. Eds. William C. DeVane and Kenneth L. Knickerbocker. New Haven: Yale University Press, 1950.

D. Bibliographies

Barnes, Warner. *A Bibliography of Elizabeth Barrett Browning.* Austin and Waco: University of Texas Press and Baylor University, 1967.

Ehrsam, Theodore G., Robert H. Deily, and Robert M. Smith. *Bibliographies of Twelve Victorian Authors.* New York: The H. W. Wilson Co., 1936.

Faverty, Frederic E. *The Victorian Poets: A Guide to Research.* 2nd ed.

Cambridge: Harvard University Press, 1969.

Peterson, William S. *Robert and Elizabeth Barrett Browning: An Annotated Bibliography, 1951-1970.* New York: The Browning Institute, 1974.

Wise, Thomas J. *A Bibliography of the Writings in Prose and Verse of Elizabeth Barrett Browning.* London: Printed for pviate circulation by Richard Clay and Sons, 1918.

—. *A Browning Library.* London: Printed for Private Circulation, 1929.

E. Thomas J. Wise's Work and Exposure

Carter, John, and Graham Pollard. *An Enquiry Into the Nature of Certain Nineteenth Century Pamphlets.* 1934; rpt. New York: Haskell House, 1971.

Gosse, Edmund. "Critical Kit-Kats," *Collected Essays of Edmund Gosse.* Vol. III. New York: Charles Scribner's Sons, 1914.

Nicoll, William Robertson and Thomas J. Wise. *Literary Anecdotes of the Nineteenth Century.* Vol. II. 1895; rpt. New York: AMS Press Inc., 1967.

Partington, Wilfred G. *Thomas J. Wise in the Original Cloth.* London: Robert Hale, 1947.

Pedley, Katherine Greenleaf. *Moriarty in the Stacks.* Berkeley: Peacock Press, 1966.

Peterson, William S. *Interrogating the Oracle.* Athens: Ohio University Press, 1969.

Todd, William B., Ed. *Thomas J. Wise: Centenary Studies.* Austin: University of Texas Press, 1959.

F. Works on Bibliography and Textual Criticism

Bowers, Fredson. *Textual and Literary Criticism.* Cambridge: Cambridge University Press, 1959.

Brack, O. M., Jr., and Warner Barnes, Eds. *Bibliography and Textual Criticism.* Chicago: University of Chicago Press, 1969.

Robson, John M., Ed. *Editing Nineteenth-Century Texts.* Toronto: University of Toronto Press, 1967.

Statement of Editorial Principles and Procedures. New York: Modern Language Association of America, 1972.

Thorpe, James, and Claude M. Simpson, Jr. *The Task of the Editor.* Los Angeles: Clark Library, 1969.

INDEX

Arnold, Matthew, x

Bagni di Lucca, xix-xx
Barnes, Warner, xxvii
Barrett Moulton-Barrett, Arabel, xxvi
Barrett Moulton-Barrett, Edward (father), xiii-xiv, 144*n*, 156*n*
Barrett Moulton-Barrett, Edward (brother), vii, xi, xiii-xiv, 94*n*
Barrett Moulton-Barrett, Elizabeth (shortened by herself to Elizabeth Barrett Barrett, frequently abbreviated to E.B.B., the initials she normally used in signing prose and poetry contributions to various contemporary journals); condition when she met Browning, x *et passim;* distrust of love, 139-140*n*; early life, vii, 93-94*n*; feelings about Edward's death, xiii-xiv; feelings towards father, xiii-xiv; image of herself during composition of *Sonnets,* 13*n*, 27-28*n*, 49-50*n*, 53*n,* and throughout *Sonnets;* nickname, 115, 115*n*; Poetry:
Aurora Leigh, xvii, 152*n*, 165
"Cowper's Grave," ix
"Cry of the Children," ix
"Cyprus Wine," ix
Dream of Exile, viii
"Lady of the Brown Rosarie," viii
"Lord Walter's Wife," ix
"Man's Requirements," ix
"Night and the Merry Man," ix
"Past and Future," ix, 23*n*, 147*n*
Poems, 1844, xix, xxii, xxiv
Poems, 1850, xx, xxi-xxv
Poems, 1853, xxi-xxii, xxiv-xxv, xxviii*n*
Poems, 1856, xxi-xxii, xxiv-xxvi
Reading Sonnets, xxi-xxii
"Rhyme of the Duchess May," viii
"Romance of the Swan's Nest," ix
"Romaunt of the Page," viii
"Runaway Slave at Pilgrim's Point," ix

"Sea-Side Walk," ix
Seraphim, viii
Sonnets from the Portuguese, British Library MS of, xvii-xviii, xxiii; copy-text for, xxiv-xxvi, 148*n*; critical opinion of, xv-xvii; first publication of, xx-xxi; first shown to Browning, xix-xx; Houghton MS of, xxiii, xxiv, 148*n*, 152*n*, 159*n*; ironic reversal of Browning in, xi, 9*n*, 27*n*, 41*n*, 57*n*, 131*n*; Morgan MS of, xxii-xxiii, 61*n*, 148*n*; Reading Sonnets, xxi-xxii; reason for name of, xx; revision of, xxiv-xxvi; texts for variorum, xxii; time of composition, xi; uniqueness in E.B.B.'s work, vii, x, xv
"Student," ix
"To Bettine," ix
"To Flush, My Dog," ix
"Vanities," ix
"Vision of Poets," viii
"Young Queen," ix
quality of mind, viii; reaction to Browning's first letter, xix; relationship between correspondence and *Sonnets,* x-xv, xix, throughout notes; religious feelings, vii-ix; social and political interests, ix, xv;
Bayne, Peter, xx
Boyd, Hugh Stuart, vii, ix
Brack, O. M., Jr., xxvii*n*
Browning, Elizabeth Barrett, see Barrett Moulton-Barrett, Elizabeth
Browning, Robert, vii, x; and the Barretts, xiii-xiv; as portrayed in *Sonnets,* 13*n*; beginning of correspondence with E.B.B., xix; his letters as source for elements in *Sonnets,* xi, 9*n*, 27*n*, 41*n*, 57*n*, 131*n*; involvement in publication of *Sonnets,* xx, xxiv-xxvi; sees *Sonnets* first time, xix-xx
Browning, Sarianna, xxiv, xxvii*n*
Byron, George Gordon, 6th Baron, 5*n*

Carter, John, xxi-xxii, xxvii*n*
Chapman, Edward, xxiv, xxv, xxvi
Clark, William Andrews, 151*n*
Clarke, Helen, xxx, 1*n*, 31*n*, 37*n*, 53*n*, 63*n*, 67*n*, 129*n*, 140*n*
Curle, Richard, xxvii*n*

De Vane, William C., xxvii*n*

Electra, xii, 17, 17*n*

Forster, John, xxvii*n*

Index 173

Greg, W. W., xxvii*n*

Hayter, Alethea, xv-xvi, xviii*n*
Hood, Thurman L., xxvii*n*
Hunt, Leigh, xx

Johnson, Samuel, 5*n*, 9*n*, 33*n*

Kaplan, Cora, xvii, xviii*n*
Kenyon, John, xxvii*n*
Kintner, Elvan, xviii*n*, xxix, 17*n*, 50*n*
Knickerbocker, Kenneth L., xxvii

Markus, Julia, xvii, xviii*n*

Peterson, William S., xiv, xvii, xviii*n*, 63*n*
Petrarch, vii
Pindar, 67, 67*n*
Pliny, 17*n*
Pollard, Graham, xxi-xxii, xxvii
Porter, Charlotte, xxx, 1*n*, 31*n*, 37*n*, 53*n*, 63*n*, 67*n*, 129*n*, 140*n*

Ratchford, Fannie, xxix

Sand, George, viii
Shakespeare, William, vii, 151-152*n*
Shelley, Percy Bysshe, viii-ix, xvii
Sophocles, xii, 17*n*

Taplin, Gardner, xv, xvi, xviii*n*
Theocritus, 1, 1*n*

Wedgwood, Julia, xx
Wise, Thomas J., xxii
Woolf, Virginia, viii, xv, xvi, xviii*n*
Wordsworth, William, vii

A Variorum Edition

of

Elizabeth Barrett Browning's

Sonnets from the Portuguese

Composed in IBM Selectric Composer Aldine Roman and Journal Roman *and printed offset, sewn and bound by Braun and Brumfield, Incorporated, Ann Arbor, Michigan. The paper on which the book is printed is Warren's* "1854."

A Variorum Edition of Elizabeth Barrett Browning's Sonnets from the Portuguese *is a Trenowyth book, the scholarly publishing division of The Whitston Publishing Company.*

This edition consists in 500 casebound copies.

2106